Collins

Reflective Project

Student Handbook

Wilma Shen and Becky Youngman

For the IB Career-related Programme

William Collins' dream of knowledge for all began with the publication of his first book in 1819.
A self-educated mill worker, he not only enriched millions of lives, but also founded a flourishing publishing house.
Today, staying true to this spirit, Collins books are packed with inspiration, innovation and practical expertise.
They place you at the centre of a world of possibility and give you exactly what you need to explore it.

Published by Collins
An imprint of HarperCollins*Publishers*
The News Building, 1 London Bridge Street, London, SE1 9GF, UK

HarperCollins*Publishers*
Macken House, 39/40 Mayor Street Upper, Dublin 1, D01 C9W8, Ireland

Browse the complete Collins catalogue at
collins.co.uk

© HarperCollins*Publishers* Limited 2026

10 9 8 7 6 5 4 3 2 1

A catalogue record for this publication is available from the British Library.

ISBN 978-0-00-877025-9

All rights reserved. No part of this publication may be reproduced, stored in a retrieval system, or transmitted in any form by any means, electronic, mechanical, photocopying, recording or otherwise, without the prior written permission of the Publisher or a licence permitting restricted copying in the United Kingdom issued by the Copyright Licensing Agency Ltd, 5th Floor, Shackleton House, 4 Battle Bridge Lane, London SE1 2HX.

Without limiting the exclusive rights of any author, contributor or the publisher of this publication, any unauthorised use of this publication to train generative artificial intelligence (AI) technologies is expressly prohibited. HarperCollins also exercise their rights under Article 4(3) of the Digital Single Market Directive 2019/790 and expressly reserve this publication from the text and data mining exception.

Authors: Wilma Shen and Becky Youngman
Publisher: Catherine Martin
Senior Product Developer: Daniela Mora Chavarría
Development editor: Sonya Newland
Copyeditor: Mark Gadd
Proofreader: Catherine Dakin
Cover designer: Amparo Barreras (Kneath Associates)
Typesetter and illustrator: Six Red Marbles
Production controller: Alhady Ali
Printed and Bound in the UK by Ashford Colour Ltd.

Acknowledgements
With thanks to Christopher Baker Raivo for their review comments.

The publishers gratefully acknowledge the permission granted to reproduce the copyright material in this book. Every effort has been made to trace copyright holders and to obtain their permission for the use of copyright material. The publishers will gladly receive any information enabling them to rectify any error or omission at the first opportunity.

We are grateful to the International Baccalaureate Organization for their permission to reproduce copyright material under licence, including the Aims of the Reflective Project, the IB Learner Profile, the Approaches to Learning (ATL) skills, the Structure and stages of the Reflective Project, the Relationship of the Reflective Project to the four elements of the Career-related Programme, the Career-related Programme model graphic, the Reflective Project assessment criteria and markbands, guidance on achievement in the Reflective Project, the definition of reflection and reflexivity, the Personal and Professional Skills (PPS) course requirements, the PPS learning outcomes, and the stages of structuring inquiries from the IB Reflective Project Guide and the Personal and Professional Skills (PPS) Guide © International Baccalaureate Organization, 2025.

This work has been developed independently from and is not endorsed by the International Baccalaureate Organization. International Baccalaureate, Baccalauréat International, Bachillerato Internacional and IB are registered trademarks owned by the International Baccalaureate Organization.

Contents

How to use this book 4

Introduction 6

| 1 | What is the reflective project? 10

| 2 | The reflective project learning journey 16

| 3 | The reflective project in context 29

| 4 | The preparation and planning phase 38

| 5 | The research and analysis phase: Research 56

| 6 | The research and analysis phase: Analysis 77

| 7 | The development phase 93

| 8 | Presenting your findings 127

| 9 | Completion and submission 135

| 10 | Your questions answered 146

Glossary 154

How to use this book

This user-friendly student handbook has been designed to help support you through each phase of the Reflective Project to allow you to tackle this challenge with confidence.

- Each chapter includes a **quick overview** of the main topics covered, to guide you through the structure:

> **This chapter covers the following:**
> - An outline of the reflective project learning journey
> - Reflective project requirements and criteria
> - The importance of reflective practice and feedback

- The main **learner profile** attributes featured are also highlighted at the forefront of each chapter and emboldened in colour within the text:

> **Learner profile traits**
> inquirers
> knowledgeable
> thinkers
> communicators
> reflective

- **Examples** showcase a range of subject areas and interdisciplinary topics and model different ways of approaching each phase of the learning journey:

> **Example**
>
> **Refining your question**
>
> Here are some examples of how to focus an ethical issue on a specific dilemma:
>
> | Issue | Initial question | Refined question |
> |---|---|---|
> | Child labour | 'How does child labour affect both the children and the economy in a country, and what is being done to prevent it?' | 'Knowing that many poor communities rely on income from all family members, should child labour be entirely illegal?' |
> | Patient confidentiality | 'What legal steps must a doctor follow when patient confidentiality conflicts with protecting others from harm?' | 'Should healthcare professionals breach patient confidentiality when it conflicts with their duty to protect others from harm?' |
> | Data privacy | 'What measures should companies implement to protect user data while maintaining business growth?' | 'Should companies prioritise protecting user data over technological innovation and business growth?' |

- **Learning journal entry** boxes support reflection and prompt you to put your learning into practice via various activities and opportunities for feedback:

> ### Learning journal entry
>
> #### Activity
>
> Use the checklist above to ensure you have met all the requirements for the reflective project. If any areas have not been addressed, reflect on the feedback you have been given to help you make any final revisions. Then use the descriptors for criteria A to D in Chapter 7 to self-assess your project.
>
> #### Reflect
>
> What final mark would you give yourself? Why?
>
> Is there anything you could still improve before you submit your project?

- **Remember** boxes highlight essential points within each chapter:

> ### Remember
>
> If you use your outline and first draft to prepare for your presentation, everything on the checklist should already be there, so check that you have considered all these ideas in your project. If you use presentation software (such as PowerPoint, Prezi, Google Slides, Sway, and so on) you can create one slide for each of the required items as an additional way of checking that you have included everything.

- **Key takeaways** checklists summarise the learning in each chapter, for easy reference:

> ### Key takeaways: Chapter 5
>
> - Research is the foundation of your reflective project. Gathering, evaluating and using information carefully helps you understand your ethical dilemma thoroughly and supports your analysis.
> - You should choose research methods that fit your topic and resources. Primary research lets you collect original data, while secondary research uses existing information. Combining both often gives the best results.
> - Evaluate your sources critically. Use tools such as the CRAAP test or OPVL method to check if your information is current, reliable, relevant and unbiased.
> - Create an annotated bibliography. Summarising and evaluating each source helps you organise your research, think critically, and justify your choices.
> - Use AI responsibly and ethically. AI can support your learning and research but should never replace your own thinking or writing. Always be transparent about your use of AI.

- **Key terms** are bolded within the text and are defined at the end of the chapter as well as in the Glossary at the end of the book:

> ### Key terms
>
> **abstract:** a summary of the contents of a piece of academic research
>
> **anecdote:** a short, sometimes amusing, account of something that has happened
>
> **call to action:** an exhortation to do something to achieve an aim or deal with a problem
>
> **dialogue tagging:** also known as speech tags, these are phrases that are used to break up sections of written dialogue (for example, 'he said')
>
> **diction:** choice of words or the manner of expression

Introduction

The reflective project (RP) is an independent, research-based, in-depth work in which you explore an ethical dilemma related to a career that you are interested in. You will work on it over an extended period of time, using your own initiative to create a thoughtful representation of your experiences and the skills you will have gained during the Career-related Programme (CP). You will be able to decide how you present your findings – in written, audio, visual or audio-visual format. This component helps you to develop critical thinking, research and professional communication skills, while considering different perspectives and contexts related to your chosen ethical dilemma. You will work closely with a supervisor, and will be challenged to think like a future career professional, developing skills that will benefit you in your future education and your career development.

The reflective project is a compulsory part of the Career-related Programme. The table below summarises some of its most important aspects.

Key aspect	Details
Focus	It must explore an ethical dilemma related to a career area. (See 'Reflective project requirements and criteria' in Chapter 2.)
Format	It may be submitted in various formats (written, audio, visual, audio-visual). (See 'Choosing your project format' in Chapter 4 for details and 'Format options for the reflective project' in Chapter 7.)
Length	It must be up to 4,000 words in total, including a written reflective statement of up to 1,000 words. (See 'Reflective project requirements and criteria' in Chapter 2, 'Format options for the reflective project' in Chapter 7 and 'Completing and submitting your written reflection' in Chapter 9.)
Time	It requires a minimum of 50 hours of independent work. (See 'Reflective project requirements and criteria' in Chapter 2.)
Supervision	You will receive 3–6 hours of support from your reflective project supervisor, including a viva voce (a concluding interview). (See 'Working effectively with your supervisor' in Chapter 1)
Presentation	You will present your research findings and receive feedback after your first draft. (See 'Presenting your findings' in Chapter 8.)
Viva Voce	You will participate in a concluding interview with your supervisor at the end of the process. (See 'Preparing for and participating in your viva voce' in Chapter 9.)
Assessment	Your reflective project is submitted to the IB for assessment. It is assessed using five criteria that are aligned with assessment objectives. (See 'Reflective project requirements and criteria' in Chapter 2 and 'Using the assessment criteria to self-evaluate your project' in Chapter 7.)
Passing requirement	You must achieve at least a D grade to be eligible for the IB Career-related Programme Certificate.

The aims of the reflective project

The aims of the reflective project are for you to:

- engage in personal inquiry
- develop critical-thinking and research skills to explore an ethical dilemma
- seek and appreciate local and/or global perspectives
- appraise the reliability and bias of resources found during the research process
- develop effective communication skills by creating a structured, coherent and balanced argument.
- develop self-management skills to support the research, writing and product-creation process
- engage in ongoing reflective practice.

The IB learner profile and approaches to learning for the reflective project

The reflective project is an independent research project that brings together everything you have learned as an IB student in a holistic way. As part of this learning journey, you will engage deeply with your own interests and ethical considerations, developing knowledge and the attributes and skills necessary for lifelong learning and global citizenship.

The IB learner profile

The IB learner profile consists of ten key characteristics that all the International Baccalaureate Programmes are designed to help you nurture and develop. These traits will help you become more well-rounded, empathetic, confident and self-aware, and equip you with valuable skills that extend well beyond the classroom. All the IB learner profile attributes are fundamental to the reflective project process.

The IB learner profile

The aim of all IB programmes is to develop internationally minded people who, recognising their common humanity and shared guardianship of the planet, help to create a better and more peaceful world.

Reflective project context

IB learners strive to be:

Inquirers: In the reflective project, you will actively engage in personal inquiry, take initiative to formulate your own research question, and independently explore an ethical dilemma related to your career interest. You will pursue knowledge, develop sustained inquiry skills, and demonstrate enthusiasm for learning throughout your reflective project and beyond the classroom.

Knowledgeable: You will draw on a broad base of knowledge to investigate your chosen ethical dilemma, connecting it to broader local or global contexts to enhance the depth of your analysis. This ensures your project is grounded in well-researched understanding relevant to your field.

Thinkers: The reflective project will challenge you to critically analyse complex ethical dilemmas, evaluate multiple perspectives and sources for potential bias, and make thoughtful, principled decisions about your personal position and your research approach.

Communicators: You will communicate your research findings and reflections clearly and effectively through your chosen format, demonstrating clarity, coherence and creativity. You will also engage in meaningful dialogue with your supervisor, peers and other community members.

Principled: Ethics is central to the reflective project. You must approach your research with integrity, respect intellectual property and take responsibility for your own work. You will also explore the ethical dilemma with careful planning and a considered approach, reflecting on your own values and the ethical implications of your personal stance.

Open-minded: The reflective project requires you to consider a range of viewpoints on your ethical dilemma, to challenge your own assumptions and biases, and to demonstrate openness to new ideas and cultural perspectives throughout your research. You will also consider any feedback you receive with an open mind.

Caring: You will reflect on the human and societal impact of your ethical dilemma, showing empathy and a commitment to make a positive difference through your proposed actions.

Risk-takers: The reflective project encourages you to step beyond your comfort zone by tackling complex ethical questions, sometimes to challenge deeply entrenched social norms and traditions – and to confidently defend your conclusions. You may also be challenged to manage the complex tasks of a lengthy independent project for the first time or to explore a new format to communicate your findings.

Balanced: Managing the reflective project alongside other academic and personal commitments requires you to develop effective time-management and self-care strategies to maintain balance throughout the process. You will also be required to maintain a balanced focus within your project as you explore a variety of different perspectives.

Reflective: Reflective practice is integral to the reflective project, as you continuously evaluate your research process, decisions and personal growth, documenting insights in your learning journal and in the final written reflection.

Approaches to learning skills

The IB approaches to learning help you build skills to become a better learner in all your IB classes. It focuses on five important skill areas – how you think, communicate, work with others, manage yourself, and research. Instead of teaching these skills separately, your teachers work them into all your subjects. This creates a shared language across your classes and supports you in becoming a more curious, knowledgeable and caring individual – qualities that will benefit you throughout your life and help you make a positive difference in the world. The reflective project provides a unique opportunity for you to develop and apply the approaches to learning skills in an authentic context.

Approaches to learning skills
Reflective project context

Thinking skills: In the reflective project, you will critically analyse the complex ethical dilemma you have identified, explore multiple perspectives, and apply your knowledge across different contexts. You will employ critical and creative thinking to identify innovative and sensible solutions to your dilemma and to develop your project. You will reflect continuously on your learning process to refine your inquiry and develop deeper understanding.

Social skills: Although the reflective project is an independent piece of work, you will collaborate with your supervisor and peers for guidance and feedback, or reach out to other school or community members for support. You will manage challenges constructively and demonstrate emotional and intellectual resilience throughout the research process.

Communication skills: Effective communication is essential in the reflective project as you articulate your ideas clearly and coherently through your chosen format. You will listen and respond to feedback, and use traditional or digital tools to research and share your work.

Self-management skills: You will plan and organise your project timeline, maintain motivation and focus despite challenges, manage stress, and reflect on your learning and personal growth to successfully complete the reflective project. You will develop the independence and self-regulation critical for lifelong learning.

Research skills: You will independently plan and conduct research, gather and evaluate sources critically and ethically, synthesise information, and communicate findings effectively in your reflective project. You will demonstrate responsible use of media and information throughout your project. In addition, you will accurately cite all sources used, ensuring proper acknowledgment of original authors and ideas.

Chapter 1 – What is the reflective project?

This chapter covers the following:
- Definition and purpose of the reflective project
- Connections to the rest of your studies
- Working effectively with your supervisor

Learner profile traits
inquirers
knowledgeable
thinkers
communicators
reflective

Definition and purpose of the reflective project

The reflective project (RP) is one of the four core components of the Career-related Programme. It is a research project – but more than that, it is a learning journey that gives you the opportunity to make connections across all your studies, and to dive deeper into a topic that interests you.

The reflective project is unique because it is based on the exploration of an **ethical dilemma** related to a career field that you are passionate about. You will look at different sides to the dilemma, consider how it affects the various organisations or individuals involved, and develop your own viewpoint – all valuable real-world skills.

Keeping a learning journal

This book guides you step-by-step through your reflective project journey. One of the most important tools is your learning journal. Think of this as a personal space to jot down important notes and ideas as you work through your project. This ongoing activity shows your learning progress and encourages genuine and sustained reflective practice. It supports your reflective project development and upholds academic integrity.

There is no single 'right' way to maintain your learning journal – you can use whatever format feels best for you. That might be a notebook, a digital space, a blog or a mix of different tools. You might include written entries, drawings, voice notes, photos, or anything else that helps you express your ideas.

Your learning journal can include:

- thoughts and questions
- research notes and discoveries
- feedback from your supervisor, peers, mentors and other community members
- reflections on the different stages of your reflective project learning journey
- plans and ideas for actions you will take.

How this book will help

Throughout this book, you will find:

- prompts and activities to inspire reflections on the work you have done and keep you moving forward
- tools and templates to help you organise your thoughts

- examples of other students' work to show you what various features of the reflective project might look like
- examples of the learner profile traits and approaches to learning skills you will demonstrate at different stages of the project, helping you to recognise and build important skills such as **critical thinking**, communication and self-management.

This book is designed to guide you through every phase of the reflective project, and prepare you for milestones such as the oral presentation of your research findings, the writing of your first draft and final project, your final reflection, and the concluding interview with your supervisor.

> ## Remember
> Your learning journal is not graded, so don't stress about making it perfect. Use it as a safe and free space to explore, experiment and grow as a student. By the end of your reflective project, you will have a record of your entire learning journey that you can be proud of!

Connections to the rest of your studies

The reflective project is a culminating learning experience – think of it as the final showcase of your studies, where everything comes together.

Most schools begin the reflective project a few months into the first year of the Career-related Programme, but the exact timing depends on your school's schedule. By the time you start on your reflective project journey, you will already have acquired a broad base of knowledge and skills. You might be wondering how this big project fits in with the whole CP journey. The answer is: more than you might think! In fact, the reflective project links to all parts of the Career-related Programme.

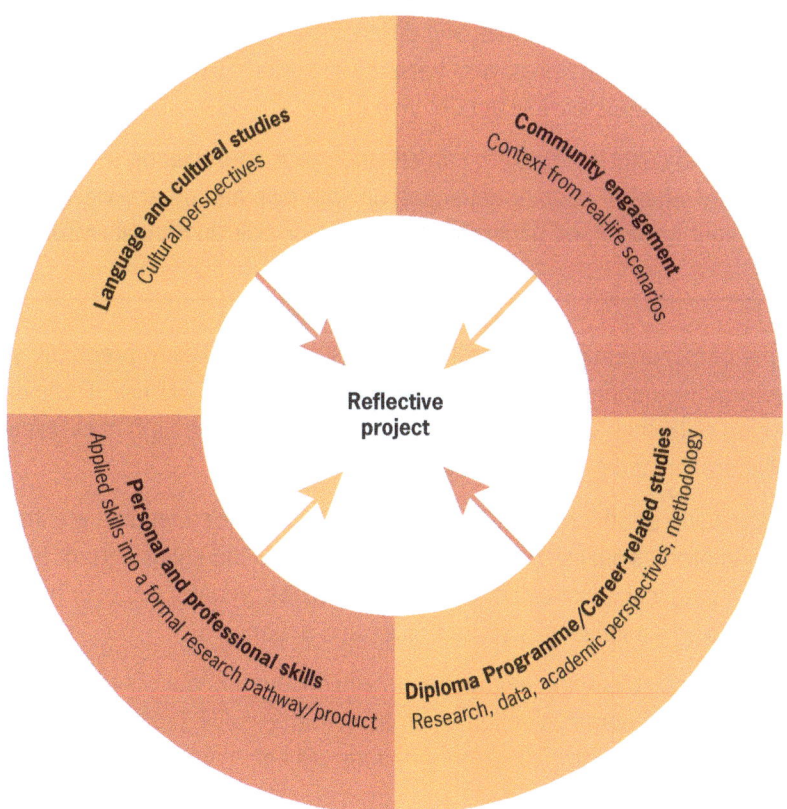

As you engage with your studies in the Career-related Programme, you will notice that each component offers opportunities to explore different ethical dilemmas, enhance your **ethical thinking** and **ethical decision-making** skills, and improve your intercultural understanding. Each of the core components will also help you develop the critical-thinking skills required to successfully complete the reflective project.

Community engagement

Community engagement (CE) is your chance to take what you have learned in the classroom and apply it in a real-world setting. Whether you are volunteering, helping in your community or working on community projects, these experiences help you understand community needs, engage with others and appreciate diverse **perspectives**.

You may have already encountered real-life ethical dilemmas related to your community. For example, you might have seen refugees or migrant workers being treated unfairly, or you may have noticed that minority voices often get overlooked. These experiences can help you identify ethical issues and understand their impact on various individuals, groups or communities.

The reflective project encourages you to think like a future practitioner in the area you are exploring, and the practical nature of community engagement can help you bridge research and real-life applications. Sound ethical decisions require research, **thinking** skills and effective **communication**. Depending on your ethical dilemma and research topic, you might consider involving **stakeholders** from your community engagement activities to gather a variety of perspectives through surveys, questionnaires and interviews.

Language and cultural studies

Language and cultural studies (LCS) can help you develop different cultural perspectives for examining ethical dilemmas. By exploring how language and culture shape the way people think and act, you will discover new perspectives and deepen your understanding of ethical issues. Analysing written materials, dialogues and narratives can reveal similarities and differences across cultures. For example, you might find that ideas about freedom of expression vary between cultures. This kind of insight will help you reflect on your own views and appreciate others' points of view.

Understanding linguistic and cultural **contexts** can enhance your appreciation of how ethical dilemmas are formed and interpreted by different people. Reflecting on your own and others' viewpoints regarding ethical dilemmas will improve your intercultural understanding and your skills in critical **reflexive** practice.

Personal and professional skills

Your experience in the personal and professional skills (PPS) course is key to preparing you for the research skills and **reflective** practice needed throughout your reflective project journey. Throughout the PPS course, you will develop skills that are essential for this process, such as time-management, research, communication, collaboration and critical thinking.

Developing an understanding of ethics and the ability to apply this understanding are important not only to the personal and professional skills component, but also to the entire core of the Career-related Programme. By exploring ethical questions in your PPS **inquiries**, you will discover how ethics plays a role in different situations and how it influences your choices and actions.

Additionally, through the various learning engagements you encounter, you will become familiar with different formats and modes of communication, such as written essays, business plans, presentations, videos, audio and multimedia products. These experiences will help you understand how to choose the best format for your final reflective project.

Diploma Programme subjects

The Diploma Programme subjects you are studying add another layer to your Career-related Programme experience by further developing your academic and research skills. The internal assessments (IAs) you complete in these subjects involve research and **analysis**, which is great practice for your reflective project.

The internal assessments also encourage you to consider the ethical dimensions of various human activities. For example, a Business Management course can help you examine how the hospitality industry adapts to the effects of artificial intelligence, while a Psychology course might help you understand the impact of mature topics and themes in children's television programmes.

Career-related studies (CRS)

Career-related studies (CRS) provide specialist **knowledge** about your chosen career path. This real-world focus helps you identify ethical dilemmas that professionals in your field face every day. Do not hesitate to talk to or even interview your CRS teachers – they are often experts in their fields and can give you valuable background information and ideas.

When you put together your Diploma Programme courses, career-related studies and the Career-related Programme core components, you get a strong, unique preparation for your reflective project. This mix of academic knowledge, practical experience and essential skills will help you explore your ethical dilemma in a way that is meaningful and relevant to your future career goals.

Learning journal entry

Reflection

What ethical issues or dilemmas have you encountered in your community engagement experiences?

Think about your language and cultural studies, personal and professional skills course, Diploma Programme subjects and career-related studies. Is there anything of interest that might become the focus of your reflective project?

Activity

In your learning journal, draw a mind map to show how your learning experiences in other components of the Career-related Programme curriculum could potentially connect with your reflective project and to identify how they could support your reflective project process.

Working effectively with your supervisor

Your reflective project will take place over the two years of your Career-related Programme. While you will generally be working independently, you will not be alone – there will be a supervisor to support and guide you throughout your journey. Your supervisor might be your career-related studies teacher, your Diploma Programme subject teacher, a CP core teacher, or another staff member at your school. Think of them as a mentor for your reflective project, someone who is there to help you stay on track, offer advice and cheer you on. You will have between three and six hours of meetings with your supervisor during your reflective project journey, including a final interview called a **viva voce**.

> **Remember**
>
> Your relationship with your supervisor will work best if you are proactive about it. Your supervisor is there to listen, guide and support you, but it is up to you to take the lead in keeping the communication open and making the most of your time together. Your supervisor will listen to your ideas and can keep you engaged and motivated when the project becomes challenging.

Getting the most from feedback

A key element of your interaction with your reflective project supervisor is the feedback they will give you. In the context of the reflective project, developmental feedback is not criticism or judgement – it is meant to help you improve and grow.

Throughout the reflective project journey, there are several points at which you will receive feedback from both your supervisor and your peers. The focus of this feedback will vary depending on the specific stage of your journey. For example, you might seek advice on different format options during the preparation and planning phase, or you might want feedback on the quality of your sources during the research phase. You can also initiate additional feedback opportunities at any point during your reflective project journey.

Working well with your supervisor can make your reflective project journey smoother, more enjoyable and more successful. So take initiative, stay connected and make the most of this valuable support.

> **Building a positive relationship with your supervisor**
>
> ✓ **Clear communication:** Be open about your progress and challenges. Keeping your supervisor up to date about what you need means you can work towards your goals effectively.
> ✓ **Be proactive:** Don't wait for your supervisor to come to you. Regularly update them, ask questions and seek advice. They have lots of experience and resources to help you make informed decisions.
> ✓ **Manage your time and stay flexible:** Plan your work carefully to meet deadlines and keep your project moving forward. But remember, things do not always go as planned. Be willing to adjust your approach and work with your supervisor to find solutions.
> ✓ **Welcome feedback and reflect:** Take feedback with an open mind and use it to improve. Reflect regularly on what you have learned and how you can apply it to your project.

Learning journal entry

Activity

Write down any specific areas where you feel you need support or guidance from your supervisor at this early stage of your reflective project.

Reflection

Besides your supervisor, who else can you turn to for support and guidance during your reflective project journey?

How can you create opportunities to receive feedback from your peers and other faculty members? Why might it be helpful to have multiple sources of feedback and support?

Key takeaways: Chapter 1

- The reflective project (RP) is a research-based project where you explore an ethical dilemma connected to your future career interests.
- The reflective project spans the two years of your Career-related Programme (CP) and culminates in a final project submission during your second year.
- Your reflective project learning journey is supported by connections to the other CP core components, your IB Diploma Programme (DP) courses, and career-related studies (CRS), all of which help build your skills and knowledge.
- You will work independently, but you will also have the guidance of a supervisor who mentors you throughout your reflective project journey. Building a positive relationship with your supervisor is essential for staying motivated and making steady progress.
- Feedback from your supervisor and peers is a helpful tool for growth.

Key terms

analysis: the process of considering something carefully or using statistical methods to understand or explain it

context: the circumstances, events and settings that give meaning to what is learned; context helps make sense of the world by considering the factors that influence what is seen, heard or read

critical thinking: the process of examining a subject or idea carefully and critically, without allowing yourself to be influenced by opinions or feelings

ethical decision-making: the process of choosing a course of action when faced with moral questions or dilemmas; this involves evaluating different options based on your ethical values and considering the consequences for all people affected, to arrive at a responsible and justifiable choice

ethical dilemma: an ethical issue in which someone must choose between conflicting values or actions, each with its own drawbacks; while all ethical dilemmas are ethical issues, not all ethical issues necessarily present a dilemma

ethical thinking: the process of carefully considering right and wrong, and using your values to guide your decisions; this involves critically examining your own beliefs and the possible effects of choices on others to act responsibly and fairly

perspective: a particular way of thinking about something, especially one that is influenced by someone's own beliefs or experiences

reflexivity: the ability to examine your own thoughts, feelings, beliefs, attitudes and behaviours; in the context of the reflective project, it means being aware of your own assumptions and biases, and understanding how these influence your responses and decisions

stakeholder: a person, group or community that is affected by or has an interest in something; in the reflective project, this means everyone who might be impacted, whether they are in your own community or in other parts of the world

viva voce: (Latin 'with living voice') the final session or 'interview' with your reflective project supervisor, in which you will discuss your project, the process you went through, what you learned and your personal growth

Chapter 2 – The reflective project learning journey

This chapter covers the following:
- An outline of the reflective project learning journey
- Reflective project requirements and criteria
- The importance of reflective practice and feedback

Learner profile traits
knowledgeable
thinkers
communicators
open-minded
balanced
reflective

An outline of the reflective project learning journey

The reflective project learning journey guides you through five phases:

1. Preparation and planning
2. Research and analysis
3. Development
4. Presentation of findings
5. Completion and submission.

Chapters 4–9 contain detailed information about each of these phases.

Remember
If this is your first time doing an extended independent project, it may feel overwhelming at first. But if you take it one step at a time and stay organised, you will soon grow comfortable with the process. You may even start to enjoy the freedom of being in charge of your own project!

Mirroring professional projects

The reflective project is a good way to develop skills and habits that are essential for your future learning and career. Throughout your project, you will gain experience in planning, problem-solving and managing your time – skills that are highly valued in any professional setting. Think of it as an opportunity to practise the same approaches and mindsets that you will use as a future professional when managing important projects.

Projects – whether in school, work or the community – often follow a clear structure to help people achieve their goals within a given time frame. They involve setting objectives, using different tools and strategies, and adapting to challenges along the way. In your reflective project, you will use similar methods: planning your steps, monitoring your progress and adjusting when needed. This practice helps you build confidence in your ability to organise your work and see it through to completion.

Effective project management also means keeping everyone involved and **communicating** well. Throughout your reflective project, you will keep track of your progress, seek feedback and reflect on your actions, just as professionals do in their own projects. By mirroring the structure and strategies of professional projects, your reflective project becomes a real opportunity to develop and showcase the skills that matter most in the professional setting.

Staying organised

To keep things on track, try using project management tools such as Trello, Asana or ClickUp. These apps help you create to-do lists, set deadlines, track progress and organise tasks visually. For scheduling and reminders, Google Calendar or other AI-powered tools are useful options to manage your time and incorporate important dates into your timeline. Using these tools can help you manage deadlines, organise your research and stay focused throughout your reflective project journey.

Using your learning journal

You can use your learning journal to capture your ideas, notes, experiences, feedback and reflections. You can use the 'Learning journal entry' features in this book to guide your entries. Add anything else you think is useful or important.

> ## Remember
> There is no fixed number of journal entries. The more you record, the easier it will be to draft your project, prepare for supervisor meetings, and stay on track. You can include anything you think is important – there are no limits!

> ## Learning journal entry
> ### Activity
> Use the internet or any other resources available to look up different project management tools that could help you organise your reflective project. Make a list of a few options, then pick one or two that suit your specific needs and work habits. Note down your rationale for choosing these tools.
>
> Does your school have a reflective project timeline that you need to incorporate into your own timeline? Identify a tool to help you manage your time.

Reflective project requirements and criteria

Kowing what is expected of you will help you plan and develop your project to give you the best chance of success. The following table shows a breakdown of the key elements of your reflective project.

Requirement	What it means
Ethical dilemma	Choose an ethical dilemma connected to a career field you are interested in. This is the focus of your reflective project.
Context and perspectives	Context: Make sure you use clear and relevant examples or case studies that contribute to a comprehensive understanding of the dilemma. Perspectives: Look at the dilemma from different points of view. Make sure you approach it in a fair and **balanced** way, showing the complexity of the issue.
Research	Use a wide range of sources to explore different approaches to and perspectives about the dilemma. Then, analyse them and bring together the information you find.
Personal position	Think critically about your own ideas and those of others. Based on your research, decide where you stand on the dilemma. Explain your position clearly with good reasons based on what you learned by doing your research. Think about how it might impact all the stakeholders if you were making the decision as a professional.
Clear communication	Organise your ideas in a logical way. Depending on the format you choose (essay, podcast, presentation, etc.), lay out your project using the correct stylistic and structural **conventions**.
References and citations	**Cite** your sources properly and include a **bibliography** to give proper credit. Choose a referencing style and use it consistently and correctly.
Written reflection	Show that you have thought deeply about your research and planning and **evaluate** how your project developed. Reflect on how the project helped you grow personally. The reflections from your learning journal will help with this.

Other tasks

There are several tasks that you should undertake along your reflective project journey, which are outlined in the following table. Although these are not graded by the IB, they will help you put together a successful reflective project.

Activity	What you will do
Learning journal	Keep an ongoing record of your thoughts, ideas and progress throughout your reflective project journey. This helps you reflect, stay on track and show that your work is your own. It also supports your oral presentation, final written reflection and viva voce.
Presentation	After your first draft, you will give a short (up to 10 minutes) oral presentation on your reflective project. Talk about your ethical dilemma, the different views you explored, your research, if and how your thinking changed, your personal position on the dilemma and how this might affect yours and others' future.

| Viva voce | After submitting your reflective project, you will have an interview with your supervisor about your reflective project journey. You will discuss your research, why you chose your project format, how you arrived at your personal position, how you handled feedback and challenges along the way, and how you feel about your final work. |

How your reflective project will be assessed

Your reflective project is assessed in two main ways:

- **Formative assessment:** This includes your learning journal and presentation. Both the learning journal and the presentation are designed to help you prepare for the final parts of the project – the final reflection and the viva voce. Your school might choose to assess your learning journal and your presentation, but they are not assessed by the IB.
- **Summative assessment:** This is your final project and your final written reflection. These are assessed by the IB.

Your project will be assessed against five criteria, which match the learning objectives of the reflective project and indicate what qualities your finished work should demonstrate. The following table shows how each criterion corresponds to the assessment objectives.

Criterion	Assessment objectives	Why these assessment objectives?
A: Focus on the ethical dilemma	AO1: Knowledge and understanding	The identification and description of the ethical dilemma indicate **knowledge** and understanding of both the subject and the career field.
		The contextualisation of the ethical dilemma and related issues, as well as the discussion of multiple perspectives, demonstrate knowledge and understanding of the ethical dilemma, and how it has an impact on individuals or groups.
B: Knowledge and understanding through research	AO1: Knowledge and understanding	The application of research methods establishes knowledge of the subject.
	AO2: Application and analysis	The analysis and understanding of differing perspectives are evident through the discussion presented in the project.
C: Critical thinking	AO2: Application and analysis	Appropriate analysis is used to determine and discuss relevant findings.
	AO3: Synthesis and evaluation	Both analysis and synthesis are used to draw conclusions from research and reflection that lead to the development and justification of a personal position.

D: Communication of ideas	AO3: Synthesis and evaluation	There is a balanced discussion of the research findings.
	AO4: Communication of research	Ideas are communicated using appropriate **terminology**, as well as structural and stylistic conventions.
		Ideas are organised in a coherent manner.
E: Reflective practice	AO2: Application and analysis	Reflection on the research process demonstrates analysis and evaluation of actions and feedback.
	AO3: Synthesis and evaluation	Student growth and the final project are evaluated.

Before you get too far into your reflective project, familiarise yourself with the assessment criteria. Use them like a checklist to understand what is expected from you and to guide your research, planning and development. The following sections break down what you can do at different phases of your reflective project learning journey to tackle each criterion. There is more information, plus examples, in Chapters 7 and 9, to help you understand what success in these criteria looks like.

Criterion A: Focus on the ethical dilemma

This criterion looks at how well you identify an ethical dilemma connected to a career field and how deeply you explore it through different perspectives and contexts.

Questions to ask yourself:

- Have I picked an ethical dilemma that is truly a dilemma, and that fits with a career I am interested in?
- Have I looked at the ethical dilemma from several different angles?
- Am I keeping my focus on the dilemma with good examples from different situations?

The following table outlines what a successful focus on an ethical dilemma looks like.

Nature of the ethical dilemma	Your ethical dilemma is clearly and precisely defined. It could lead to several possible resolutions.
	You clearly explain how this dilemma connects to a specific career.
Perspectives	You explore different viewpoints on the dilemma fairly and thoroughly, giving each a balanced evaluation.
Focus and context	You keep a clear and steady focus on the ethical dilemma throughout your project.

Criterion B: Knowledge and understanding through research

This criterion assesses how well you use research to deepen your understanding of the ethical dilemma and its effects.

Questions to ask yourself:

- Has my research been thorough?
- Do I understand the issues connected to the ethical dilemma?
- Have I thought about how the ethical dilemma affects different people or groups in a variety of situations?

The following table outlines what successful knowledge and understanding looks like.

Research	Your research covers a wide range of sources and goes deep into the topic.
	You use many different resources to get a full picture of the dilemma.
Knowledge and understanding	Your project demonstrates that you know and understand the issues connected to your ethical dilemma.
Impact of dilemma	You clearly explain how different people, groups or situations are affected by the dilemma, showing a strong understanding of its impact.

Criterion C: Critical thinking

This criterion looks at how well you have analysed your research and put it all together to form and explain your own position on the ethical dilemma. It also checks if you have thought about how your position might affect different people and situations.

Questions to ask yourself:

- Have I carefully analysed and synthesised my research?
- Have I clearly decided where I stand on the ethical dilemma?
- Have I explained and supported my position with good reasons?
- Have I thought about how my position might impact others?

The following table outlines what successful critical thinking looks like.

Analysis and synthesis of research	You have thoroughly analysed and synthesised your research.
	You discuss important findings clearly and effectively.
Personal position: reasoning and evidence	You clearly state your personal position.
	Your position is backed up by strong, well-focused reasoning linked to carefully chosen evidence.
Personal position: justification and impact	You provide a clear and convincing explanation for your position.
	You show that you have seriously thought about how your position might affect different people or groups.

Criterion D: Communication of ideas

This criterion looks at how well you organise your ideas and use the right language and structure to share your thoughts clearly and effectively.

Questions to ask yourself:

- Have I used the right terms and structure to explain my ideas in the best way possible?
- Are my ideas easy to follow and well organised so people understand me clearly?

The following table outlines what successful communication of ideas looks like.

Terminology	You use relevant terms and style choices consistently and correctly to help get your ideas across.
Structure	Your project is presented in a way that makes your ideas clear and easy to follow.
Development and organisation of ideas	Your ideas are well explained and organised in a logical, easy-to-understand manner.

Criterion E: Reflective practice

This criterion looks at how well you show that you've thought about and learned from your project as you planned, researched and completed it.

Questions to ask yourself:

- Have I demonstrated reflective practice?
- Have I reflected on my learning and the choices I made?
- Have I thought about how this project has affected me and might affect others?
- Have I critically looked at my own and others' ideas, actions or decisions?

The following table outlines what successful reflective practice looks like.

Reflection on process	Your reflections explain your decisions, actions and thinking clearly, and most of them are well justified.
Reflection on project	You give a detailed evaluation of how well your project worked. You explain what worked well and what did not.
Reflection on learning	You thoroughly discuss how your learning and new understandings have impacted you and others.

Learning journal entry

Activity

Think about how you will use the reflective project requirements and criteria to guide your project and research plan, and make some notes. Here are some questions to get you started:

- How will the project requirements and criteria shape the way you approach your reflective project and plan your research?
- Do any requirements seem particularly challenging? How do you plan to tackle those requirements?
- What goals do you want to set for yourself during the planning phase? How will these goals help guide what you do during the next phases of your project?

The importance of reflective practice and feedback

Reflective practice involves both **reflection** and reflexivity, which are key parts of your reflective project. While reflection focuses on learning from your actions, decisions and experiences, reflexivity goes further by examining your beliefs and values, or why you act or think in a certain way. In your reflective project, you will explore different viewpoints on your ethical dilemma and think critically about your own ideas alongside others'. This ongoing active process is central to all your learning and helps you develop as a careful and responsible **thinker**. It is also one of the main things you will be assessed on in Criterion E.

There are different types of reflection and reflexivity:

- **Definition:** Being aware of your own thinking and learning processes by examining your thoughts, actions and goals.
- **Focus:** Understanding the *how* of your learning.
- **Outcome:** Greater awareness of cognitive processes, enabling you to set goals, monitor progress and improve future learning (self-regulated learning).

Metacognitive reflection

- **Definition:** Reflecting on a past experience to draw out new or changed understandings, insights or actions.
- **Focus:** Starting with a specific event and exploring its implications
- **Outcome:** Ability to learn from experiences and decide what to do differently next time.

Process reflection

- **Definition:** Linking reflection with analytical and critical thinking.
- **Focus:** Considering your actions and experiences in broader social, cultural or historical contexts.
- **Outcome:** Recognition of complexity, multiple perspectives and deeper insights into your choices.

Critical reflection

- **Definition:** Examining your own perspective or position in a situation.
- **Focus:** Identifying and questioning *assumptions*, biases and attitudes, and seeing how your background and beliefs influence your responses.
- **Outcome:** Greater awareness of how your views affect your actions and interactions, as well as their impact on others in interconnected relationships.

Self-reflexivity

- **Definition:** Looking beyond the individual to examine collective assumptions, values and shared ways of thinking.
- **Focus:** Understanding cultural, societal and historical influences on perceptions and behaviours.
- **Outcome:** Recognition of how shared perspectives shape actions and impact others, and the ability to challenge these viewpoints to foster change in the future.

Critical reflexivity

Remember

Beyond the reflective project, these skills are valuable tools for your personal growth and future career, helping you think critically, understand others better, and make well-informed decisions throughout your life. They will serve you well far beyond school or college!

How your learning journal supports your reflective practice

Reflection is an automatic part of learning, and you probably do it regularly without realising it. However, since the reflective project is completed over the two years of your Career-related Programme studies, you should record your reflections so you can go back to them at the end of the project. Your learning journal provides a space for you to capture your reflections continuously throughout the process. You should regularly record your reflections, feedback, ideas and learning experiences. At the end, you will create a final written reflection and discuss your learning with your supervisor during the viva voce.

Remember

This book provides prompts to help you reflect on your work throughout the process. Your supervisors will also support you in understanding why reflection and reflexivity matter. As you become more comfortable with the process of reflection, you will find your own ways to think deeply, helping you grow into a more reflective and responsible student and future professional.

> ## Learning journal entry
> ### Reflection
> How can keeping a learning journal help you improve your reflective practice throughout the reflective project?

The importance of feedback

Feedback is a powerful tool for improvement, encouraging you to think critically about your actions and decisions. During your reflective project, you will receive developmental feedback that gives you clear, practical advice on how to improve your project and communicate your thinking. Giving, receiving and responding to feedback is a skill you will use throughout your life. You are encouraged to seek feedback regularly and use it to reflect and improve.

The following table makes some suggestions for when you might ask for feedback and who can help.

Learning journey phase	What to get feedback on	Who to ask
Preparation and planning	Identification of an ethical dilemma Research question Project proposal Planning research methodology Contexts and perspectives related to your identified ethical dilemma Format choices	Supervisor Peers DP, CRS and CP core teachers Librarians Other faculty and community members
Research and analysis	Research approach Resource validity Research findings Research analysis Personal position Progress on project timeline	Supervisor Peers Librarians Other faculty and community members
Development	Quality of your work Clarity of communication and structure of ideas Anything you need guidance and support on for the production of your first draft	Supervisor Peers Librarians Other faculty and community members

Presentation	Clarity and coherence of your argument Quality of your research The inclusion of the required elements Effectiveness of organisation Communication of ideas	Supervisor Peers Other faculty and community members
Completion and submission	Revision of the final draft Self-evaluation of the project output Final reflection Viva voce	Supervisor Peers

Remember

You can ask your supervisor for feedback whenever you need it. When receiving feedback, approach it with an **open mind**, as an opportunity for improvement. Note, however, that your supervisor will provide formal and detailed feedback on only *one* draft of your reflective project before your final submission. You are expected to work independently on subsequent drafts based on this feedback. Remember that receiving feedback does not necessarily mean you must act on it; consider first how it aligns with your goals and overall project progress.

How to get the most out of feedback

- ✓ **Listen carefully:** Pay close attention and take notes so you do not forget important points.
- ✓ **Keep an open mind:** Feedback is not a personal attack or criticism on your work – it is a chance to improve your project.
- ✓ **Know your own work:** Before getting feedback, look at your own work and think about what you did well and what could be better. You might focus on this to ask for feedback on a specific topic.
- ✓ **Ask questions:** If something is not clear, do not hesitate to ask for explanation or clarification.
- ✓ **Make a plan:** If the feedback you receive seems actionable, turn that feedback into specific steps you will take to improve, and track your progress.
- ✓ **Say thanks:** Showing appreciation makes people more likely to give you helpful feedback in the future. It also shows good manners and will help you improve your interpersonal skills.

Learning journal entry

Activity

Write a paragraph explaining why feedback is important in your reflective project journey and what steps you will take to reflect on the feedback you receive.

How to give others meaningful feedback

- ✓ **Be specific:** Do not just say that something is 'good' or 'bad'. Explain why and give examples.
- ✓ **Focus on improvement:** Point out areas that could be improved, and offer suggestions on how to make them better.
- ✓ **Be honest but kind:** Critique the work, not the person. For example, say 'The introduction could be clearer if you add…' instead of 'Your writing is not good'.
- ✓ **Use a feedback method:** Create a positive and productive feedback experience by using tried and trusted methods.
- ✓ **Own your opinion:** Start your feedback with 'I think…' or 'From my perspective…' to show it is your opinion and invite discussion.
- ✓ **Ideation of solutions:** Help the person you are giving feedback to think about ways to fix the problem and get even better. Inspire them!

Example

Feedback methods

Here are some example feedback methods you can try.

Feedback sandwich

This method involves layering feedback between two pieces of positive feedback (positive / area for improvement / positive). Start with something the person did well, then provide your constructive feedback on areas for improvement, and finish with another positive comment.

GROW (goal / realities / options / way forward)

This framework helps structure feedback conversations by stating the goal (understanding what the person wants to achieve), then the reality (exploring their current situation and challenges), followed by options (discussing different approaches or solutions available), and finally the way forward (exploring specific actions and next steps).

Stop / Keep / Start

This action-oriented method provides clear direction by asking three questions:

- Stop: What actions should they discontinue?
- Keep: What are they doing well that should continue?
- Start: What new actions would be beneficial?

Stanford method

This approach frames feedback constructively:

- 'I like': Positive feedback about what's working well.
- 'I wish': Developmental feedback phrased as hopes for improvement.
- 'What if': Suggestions for new possibilities or alternatives.

Ladder of feedback

This protocol builds feedback through a structured sequence:

- Clarity: Ask questions to ensure you understand their work.
- Value: Highlight what you find impressive or valuable.
- Concerns: Share worries or potential issues respectfully.
- Suggest: Offer specific ideas or suggestions for improvement.

(From Harvard Project Zero, McFarland, D. 2006)

Learning journal entry

Reflection

Reflection on process:

- What does reflective practice mean to you?
- How can you apply reflective practice in your daily life and studies?
- How do you plan to document your reflections and the feedback you receive in your learning journal?

Reflection on learning:

- What challenges might you face in implementing reflective practice and seeking feedback?
- What strategies can you use to overcome these challenges and stay committed to your reflective project journey?

Reflection on feedback:

- Recall a time when feedback helped you improve. What did you learn from that experience?
- What type of feedback do you find most helpful?

Key takeaways: Chapter 2

- The reflective project learning journey is a step-by-step process that helps you explore an ethical dilemma connected to a career field, guiding you through five phases: preparation and planning, research and analysis, development, presentation and completion.
- The reflective project mirrors professional project management, encouraging you to develop skills such as planning, researching, critical thinking and communication, which will be helpful in your future studies and career.
- Keeping a detailed learning journal will help you stay organised, reflect on your progress, and prepare for important milestones like the presentation, final reflection and viva voce.
- The reflective project assessment criteria (A–E) outline what you need to focus on, including identifying an ethical dilemma, conducting thorough research, thinking critically, communicating clearly and reflecting deeply on your learning.

- Reflective and reflexive practice are essential to all learning, but especially the reflective project. They help you understand not just what you did or how you think, but why.
- Feedback is a vital part of your reflective project learning journey. Receiving and giving feedback thoughtfully will help you improve your project and develop important skills for personal and professional growth.
- Approaching the reflective project with an open mind, curiosity and a willingness to reflect and adapt will help you get the most out of this valuable learning experience.

Key terms

assumption: something that is accepted as being true or sure to happen, without any proof

bibliography: a list of articles, books and other sources that have been referenced in a piece of work

cite: to refer and give credit to someone else's work

conventions: the typical style and structure demonstrated in specific types of writing or presentations; this might include features such as headings and subheadings, the level of formality in the language used, as well as the grammar and punctuation used

evaluate: to assess or judge the quality or importance of something

formative assessment: a range of formal and informal assessment processes carried out by teachers to assess your progress; formative assessment is designed to give you feedback to help you improve as you go along

summative assessment: an assessment at the end of a learning process designed to evaluate how much you have achieved and how well you understand the subject matter

synthesis: the combination of separate elements into a whole

terminology: the specific words and phrases that are commonly used in a particular subject, field or type of writing; knowing and using the correct terminology allows you to communicate your ideas clearly and accurately

Chapter 3 – The reflective project in context

This chapter covers the following:
- The reflective project and your future career
- Understanding ethical dilemmas

Learner profile traits
thinkers
reflective

The reflective project and your future career

The reflective project connects you to your future profession by giving you a chance to explore an ethical dilemma related to a career you are interested in. You will investigate the background and history of the dilemma and see how it affects different people and groups. You will also learn what people from different cultures and communities think about the dilemma. This will help you understand its impact close to home and in the wider world. This deep understanding will provide insights into your future career and show how you can make a positive difference as a professional.

The reflective project is based on real-life situations, so your research will reflect real challenges that you might face in your professional life, not just **theoretical** situations. The knowledge you gain will guide future learning, career choices and life decisions long after you finish the project.

The IB Career-related Programme emphasises **ethics**. This means your reflective project journey will also be meaningful and is likely to leave a lasting impact on you. The ethical **thinking** skills you develop will help you make decisions throughout your education and career. Below are some stories from graduates of the Career-related Programme, describing how the reflective project has influenced their learning and choices.

Spring's story

'My reflective project was about the extent to which artists uphold the value of freedom of expression in their artworks. As someone aspiring to be an artist, I needed to consider the amount of freedom I have to create my own works. I explored various viewpoints on controversial art, and learned how different stakeholders perceive its value. Understanding how governments view artistic freedom has shaped me as a young artist entering the industry, helping me grasp the societal dynamics, social constraints and legal considerations involved.'

Riri's story

'My reflective project question was "Music can be taken from many different sources; is there a clear line between inspiration and plagiarism for composers of this age?" This was significant to me because I wanted to be a composer of the modern day, and I dwelt a lot in the grey area between inspiration and plagiarism. It is hard to create original music when so much has already been done with a limited number of notes. This ethical dilemma continues to resonate with me as I pursue composing music and sound design for video games. The reflective project process has made me question many of my compositions, especially when inspired by other composers. I have researched legal issues in music, which has helped me when job hunting, giving me extensive knowledge about how the legal side of the music industry works and helped me avoid bad and possibly exploitative contracts.'

Samantha's story 💬

'My reflective project focused on cultural appropriation in the fashion industry. Since much of my work draws inspiration from various cultures, I've become more aware of and sensitive to different perspectives on this issue. I now understand the importance of thorough research before creating my work. Engaging with individuals from the target culture has taught me how to approach my designs respectfully, ensuring I don't rely on stereotypes or exploit cultures that inspire me.'

Esha's story 💬

'I chose to explore whether restaurants should promote meat alternatives, in order to prevent global climate change. This issue was important to me because I have been a vegetarian my entire life, and my Hindu religion prioritises the moral treatment of animals. I wanted to highlight that restaurants have a social responsibility to encourage customers to adapt their diets for environmental and health benefits. After thoroughly researching the impact of meat consumption on the environment, I continue to practise vegetarianism in my personal and professional life. The reflective project process emphasises the importance of researching a topic from various perspectives to conduct a more in-depth analysis. It helped me strengthen critical research skills that transferred into my university academic writing. It also made me reflect on the content taught in universities, which often revolves around money and how food sales can impact profitability. There is less focus on teaching students about the ethical considerations involved in food production. The reflective project highlighted these issues for me, which I find particularly important in light of my career studies. The hospitality and culinary arts industry has many underlying ethical complexities that should be addressed more in university, not just through the CP. The reflective project helped me realise that, being a customer-facing field, it significantly impacts people's diets and, consequently, the environment.'

Casey's story 💬

'I investigated the ethics of sustainability and art, especially through my involvement with Trashion (turning trash into fashion). The reflective project encouraged me to consider different perspectives and factors involved in ethical art practices. In art school, discussions around ethics, such as appropriation, are common. Understanding multiple viewpoints is crucial for me as a young artist. The reflective project I explored back then still fascinates me, and I've learned to acknowledge the contributions of others in my ceramics and sculpture work, ensuring everyone involved receives credit for their hard work.'

Audrey's story 💬

'I decided to dive into the ethical dilemma surrounding the use of technology (robots, AI and service automation) in the hospitality industry, and how it might contradict the essence of the industry. This topic continues to resonate deeply with me, as I gain real-world experience through my studies and internships. I wonder how we can use digital tools to elevate guest experiences while preserving the warmth and personal touch essential to hospitality. The reflective project has impacted how I approach ethical considerations both personally and professionally. It taught me to be mindful of how we embrace technology, ensuring it aligns with the core values of our industry. As I evaluate digital marketing strategies, or automation in service operations, I think beyond just efficiency and consider how these decisions influence guest relationships and maintain the hotels' brand identity. One of the most valuable skills I picked up during the reflective project was critical thinking. Learning to analyse different perspectives and anticipate the potential consequences of my decisions has been invaluable. I believe that the CP's focus on ethics and applied ethics has given me a unique perspective compared to my peers. It pushed me to look beyond surface-level business strategies and consider the long-term implications of choices a business makes. In today's rapidly changing industry, this is an incredibly important mindset to have. I see it as a strong asset as I continue to develop my career, enabling me to approach challenges with a sense of responsibility and care.'

Haylie's story

'My reflective project examined the ethical dilemma of the objectification of women in modern media, emphasising social equality and justice. This expanded my interest in how marginalised communities are perceived, and the impact of media representation on those communities. As a member of one of those communities, I strive to create work that challenges harmful narratives. My university Visual Arts projects reflected how women's bodies are often commodified in society and media. The reflective project has instilled in me a sense of social responsibility as a designer and artist, motivating me to produce work that educates and provokes necessary conversations. I now analyse the media critically, recognising how women's bodies are presented for profit. This awareness shapes my media consumption and informs the type of work I want to create, focusing on how culture influences our behaviours and identities. This way of looking at things and comparing them has definitely helped me to create a systematic way of working which I have learned to love.'

Gentle's story

'I investigated whether TV shows aimed at children aged four to seven should discuss mature topics such as violence, current affairs or discrimination. The reflective project has manifested in my life by making me feel confident in my existing knowledge, while staying open to new information that might change my perspective. It made me aware of how much the entertainment we choose to watch is affected by our personal boundaries and values. Understanding intersectionality has made it easier to engage with relevant themes in academia and everyday life. I use many skills learned from the reflective project daily, such as media analysis, organising my arguments, and figuring out how different ideas worked together. Additionally, the technical skills I developed during the reflective project, like video editing and interviewing, gave me the confidence to interview people throughout my academic career.'

Remember

As you work through this book, think about how your reflective project can be a tool for your own learning. By exploring authentic ethical dilemmas connected to your career interests, you will gain important insights that help you make responsible and thoughtful decisions both now and in the future. Taking this chance to **reflect** and learn will equip you with the skills and knowledge to make ethical choices that positively affect your career and the communities you work with both now and in the future.

Learning journal entry

Activity

Think about and make notes on the following questions.

Sources of inspiration: Which alumni story resonates with you the most, and why?

Motivation and goal-setting: How can this person's experiences inspire you to dive deeper into your own reflective project learning journey? What goals or intentions do you want to set for your learning and exploration as you start your reflective project?

Future skills and career: How might exploring real-world issues through the reflective project help build your skills as you prepare for your future career?

Understanding ethical dilemmas

Ethics is all about understanding what's right and wrong. It involves systems or sets of moral rules, principles or values that help guide our decisions. Ethical issues come up when questions of fairness, honesty, justice or **human rights** are involved. These issues can appear in many areas of life – personal, social, professional, economic and environmental.

To better understand how we approach ethical decision-making, it is helpful to know about the main branches of ethics that provide different frameworks for analysing moral situations.

Normative ethics

Normative ethics focuses on developing general principles or frameworks for working out what is morally right or wrong. It tries to establish standards of conduct and to provide guidance for making ethical decisions. The diagram below explains some of the key approaches taken by normative ethics.

Applied ethics

Applied ethics deals with the practical application of ethical principles to specific real-world issues and situations. It examines ethical dilemmas in a variety of fields.

Business ethics explores ethical issues in the business world, such as corporate social responsibility, fair trade and conflicts of interest.

Medical ethics/bioethics address ethical challenges in healthcare, including end-of-life decisions, genetic engineering and patient rights.

Environmental ethics focus on moral obligations to the natural environment and the ethical implications of human actions on ecosystems.

Professional ethics involve developing and upholding codes of conduct for specific professions, such as law, journalism, and engineering.

Ethics is important in every career. It shapes how professionals behave and make decisions. Each career has its own ethical considerations. For example, in healthcare, patient confidentiality is crucial; in business, corporate social responsibility is emphasised; and in education, academic **integrity** is paramount.

When making ethical decisions, professionals must think carefully about how their choices affect different people. Behaving ethically helps build trust and a positive reputation. But remember – ethics can vary between cultures and societies, which can make ethical decisions complicated, especially in a global workplace.

An ethical dilemma happens when you face a choice between two or more conflicting values or actions, with no clear right or wrong answer.

Classical philosophical ethical dilemmas

Looking to the past and considering some classical examples of ethical dilemmas will help to develop your ethical thinking skills. The following examples of philosophical scenarios show conflicts between moral principles, requiring individuals to make difficult decisions.

The trolley problem

A runaway trolley (train carriage) is speeding towards five people tied to the main track. On a side track, one person is tied down. You stand next to a lever: if pulled, it diverts the trolley to the side track, killing the one person but saving the five. If you do nothing, the trolley continues towards the five people (Thompson J.J., 1985). This scenario creates an ethical dilemma between two philosophical perspectives:

- Utilitarianism supports pulling the lever, as it maximises overall welfare (saving five lives at the cost of one).

- Deontology often opposes pulling the lever, arguing that causing someone's death violates moral rules (such as 'do not kill'), even if it saves more lives.

The core tension of this dilemma lies in personal responsibility. Doing nothing is passive – you allow five deaths without direct intervention. Pulling the lever is active – you become directly responsible for one death. Thus, the dilemma questions whether *causing harm* directly (killing one) is morally distinct from *allowing harm* indirectly (letting five die).

The Heinz dilemma

Heinz's wife is dying from a rare disease, but he cannot afford her medicine. Should he steal it to save her life or respect the law and let her die? This dilemma explores the conflict between legality and morality, prompting discussions about ethical justifications under desperate circumstances. (Kohlberg L., 1984)

The lifeboat dilemma

A lifeboat is stranded out at sea, overcrowded with people and at risk of sinking. The group must decide whether to sacrifice one person to save everyone else, or whether to risk everyone's lives by allowing all to stay on board. This dilemma looks at balancing individual rights with the moral weight of decisions made for the **greater good**. (Harding G., 1974)

Learning journal entry

Activity

Choose either the trolley problem, the Heinz dilemma or the lifeboat dilemma. Use ethical ideas like utilitarianism (aiming for the greatest good) or deontology (following rules) to analyse it. What would you decide? Why? Make notes in your learning journal.

Real-life ethical dilemmas

Sometimes real-life ethical dilemmas have made headlines because of their complexity and the discussions they provoke. Consider the examples below.

The Stanford Prison experiment

In 1971, psychologist Philip Zimbardo and his team conducted a study to investigate the psychological effects of perceived power and authority in a simulated prison environment located in the basement of Stanford University. The main goal was to see how quickly and intensely individuals would adapt to their assigned roles of 'guards' and 'prisoners'. However, within just a few days, alarming behaviours emerged. The 'guards' began displaying abusive actions, while the 'prisoners' experienced significant psychological distress. This experiment raised serious ethical concerns regarding the treatment of participants and the fine line between research and potential harm (Zimbardo, P. G., Haney, C., Banks, W. C., & Jaffe, D., 1973).

This ethical dilemma stemmed from two opposing viewpoints. Zimbardo and his team, taking a utilitarian approach, believed the insights gained about human behaviour in oppressive situations could benefit society, and that this justified the risks involved. On the other hand, critics argued from a deontological perspective, emphasising the researchers' duty to uphold the participants' rights and dignity, as well as the principle of doing no harm. They contended that no scientific objective could justify the distress and harm that participants experienced during the experiment.

The Challenger Space Shuttle disaster

In January 1986, National Aeronautics and Space Administration (NASA) faced intense pressure to launch the Space Shuttle Challenger on schedule. There were multiple reasons for this urgency, including political and public expectations, scheduling demands and budgetary constraints. Amid these pressures, serious concerns emerged about the shuttle's safety, particularly regarding components called O-rings (rubber seals in the solid rocket boosters). These concerns were based on previous technical problems and evidence that the seals could become brittle and fail when it was cold. Despite these warnings, NASA management decided to proceed with the launch. Tragically, just 73 seconds after liftoff, the shuttle broke apart, killing all seven crew members (NASA, 1986).

This case illustrates the conflict between prioritising safety and protecting human life (**beneficence** or **non-maleficence**) versus organisational pressures and a utilitarian approach about costs, schedules and political gains.

The Flint water crisis

Prior to 2014, the city of Flint, Michigan received its treated drinking water from Detroit's water system, sourced from Lake Huron. However, as a cost-saving measure, city officials, under state-appointed emergency management, decided to switch Flint's water source to the Flint River in April 2014. Over time, dangerous levels of lead were found in the water, and many residents – especially children – suffered from lead poisoning. The crisis significantly affected Flint's low-income and minority communities, raising issues of environmental justice and government accountability (Michigan Civil Rights Commission & Michigan Department of Civil Rights, 2017).

This dilemma involves a clash between justice – ensuring fairness and protecting vulnerable populations – and a utilitarian approach focused on financial benefit for the city. It also raised questions about government accountability and the government's ethical obligation to protect the **common good**.

Facebook's data privacy controversies

Facebook has faced repeated controversies over how it collects, uses and shares user **data**. High-profile incidents, such as the Cambridge Analytica scandal, revealed that personal information from millions of users was accessed and used for targeted advertising and political campaigns without user consent (Cadwalladr, C., 2018). These events raised ethical concerns about data protection, user consent and the responsibility of technology companies to safeguard personal information.

The ethical dilemma in Facebook's case is not simply about profit versus privacy. On the one hand, respecting individual **autonomy** and privacy means ensuring users have control over their personal information and are fully informed about how their data is used. This reflects ethical principles of **transparency**, **informed consent** and the **right to privacy**. On the other hand, Facebook's business model relies on collecting and analysing user data to improve services, personalise content and generate revenue through advertising. From a utilitarian perspective, these practices can be justified if they are seen as benefiting a wider group: enabling Facebook to offer free services to many more users, create jobs, support local economies and connect communities around the world. However, the challenge lies in how to balance these competing interests and the ethical obligations of tech companies.

Learning journal entry

Activity

Choose one of the real-life ethical dilemmas summarised above. Use the internet or any other resources available to find out a bit more about it, and about the branch of ethics it is concerned with. In your learning journal make some notes on both these things.

Reflection

Think about a time when you faced or witnessed an ethical dilemma in your personal life, school or community. For example, you might have found yourself in a situation where you became aware of someone cheating in a test, or a case of bullying or vandalism, or someone showing risky behaviours.

What choices did you have, and what did you decide? Reflect on how this experience shaped your understanding of ethics and the conflicting values involved.

What ethical issues have you noticed from media coverage or news? What ethical challenges do you expect, and what more do you hope to find out about these ethical issues?

Key takeaways: Chapter 3

- The reflective project connects you to the real world and provides insight into the challenges and opportunities of your future career.
- The lessons you learn on the reflective project journey may shape the way you think and behave, and the decisions you make in your future education, career and life.
- Ethics is important in every career, and each career has its own ethical considerations.
- Identifying ethical dilemmas is a crucial step in the reflective project.

Key terms

autonomy: the ability and freedom to make your own decisions rather than being told what to do by someone else; respecting autonomy means allowing people to control their own lives

beneficence: the act of doing good and helping others to make their lives better

common good: something that is available and accessible to everyone in a community or society, and which improves the wellbeing of all people, not just a few individuals

data: a collection or series of facts, observations or measurements, often presented in the form of numbers or letters

ethics: moral beliefs, rules and principles about right and wrong

greater good: help for the most people in society and decisions benefit the majority, even if this might not be the best for every single person; closely associated with the utilitarian branch of ethics

human rights: the basic rights that many societies believe that all people should have, and in which individuals and organisations such as governments should not interfere

informed consent: permission given by someone who understands fully what they are agreeing to

integrity: a quality characterised by being honest and sticking to moral principles

moral agent: a person who is able to distinguish right from wrong, make moral judgements and be held accountable for their actions

non-maleficence: the duty that people have, especially medical practitioners, to 'do no harm' when making decisions; it requires consideration of how actions might hurt or cause injury to people and what steps can be taken to avoid that

right to privacy: the fundamental right that people must be free from unwarranted intrusion or interference in their personal space, communications and information

theoretical: referring to things that exist only as an idea, rather than being real or actually happening

transparency: being open, honest and clear about what you are doing, allowing others to understand your actions and decisions, to build trust

utilitarianism: the idea that the morally correct course of action is the one that produces benefit for the greatest number of people

Chapter 4 – The preparation and planning phase

This chapter covers the following:
- Preparing for the reflective project
- Identifying an ethical dilemma and developing a research question
- Choosing your project format
- Identifying and understanding differing perspectives and contexts

Learner profile traits
knowledgeable
communicators
reflective

Preparing for the reflective project

The preparation and planning phase lays the foundation for your reflective project. It builds your knowledge and skills and helps you organise your approach. You deepen your understanding of ethical issues, learn research methods and develop feedback skills. Planning also means identifying an ethical dilemma, framing a research question, choosing a **methodology** and setting a timeline.

During the preparation phase, you should focus on:

- building foundational **knowledge** in applied ethics and **intercultural understanding** to support your analysis of ethical dilemmas. Much of this foundational knowledge will be developed through your Personal and Professional Skills (PPS) lessons and other CP core components, which will provide essential theoretical frameworks and practical applications for your project development.
- developing research and self-management skills that will be essential throughout your reflective project journey.
- learning feedback processes including how to give, receive and respond to feedback from your peers and reflective project supervisor
- exploring **reflection** techniques by practising different types of reflections and reflexivity that will inform and guide your learning journey (see Chapter 2)
- understanding project requirements by confirming your grasp of the reflective project criteria and expectations (see Chapters 2 and 7).

Key planning activities

Planning involves specific, strategic decisions about your reflective project. These include:

- identifying your ethical dilemma by researching career-related issues and narrowing them down to a specific dilemma of interest that presents conflicting values or courses of action
- developing your research approach by creating a comprehensive research plan and submitting a formal proposal to your supervisor
- designing your methodology by considering appropriate research methods and identifying potential resources for your study

- choosing the most suitable format for your final project
- establishing a structured schedule that ensures timely completion of all project components.

Throughout the preparation and planning phase, you will engage in peer discussions and receive supervisor feedback to help make decisions about the direction of your project.

> **Remember**
>
> Remember to document all your reflections, feedback and decisions in your learning journal. This continuous reflective practice will support your development throughout the entire reflective project journey.

Common pitfalls

There are two common pitfalls when preparing for your reflective project:

- taking a descriptive rather than an interrogative approach
- having a good research question about a controversial issue, but missing the ethical dilemma.

Descriptive versus interrogative approach

A descriptive project describes a social phenomenon or situation and will lead to a single answer, or an explanation of why the situation has arisen. An interrogative approach, by contrast, explores conflicts between values or perspectives and leads to debate, argumentation and multiple possible conclusions.

A descriptive approach...

- presents facts and information about a situation
- explains how things work or what currently happens
- leads to single, factual answers
- focuses on gathering and presenting existing knowledge
- answers questions that have clear, definitive responses

Question	Outcome
What are the current laws about data privacy in Europe?	This leads to a factual answer about existing laws.
How does plastic pollution affect marine life?	This leads to data or scientific facts about the environmental impact of plastic pollution on marine life.
What are the advantages of using artificial intelligence in the hiring process?	This leads to a presentation on existing information and knowledge on the benefits of using artificial intelligence in the hiring process.

An interrogative approach...

- examines conflicts between competing values or principles
- presents multiple perspectives on an issue
- leads to ongoing discussion and debate
- requires argumentation and evidence to support viewpoints
- addresses questions where people can agree or disagree

Question	Outcome
Should parents control their children's social media use?	This invites debate about the balance between children's privacy and safety, exploring different perspectives on parental responsibility, children's rights and the impact of social media.
Should healthcare workers be required to treat patients whose lifestyle choices contribute to their illness?	This examines ethical dilemmas in healthcare, such as fairness, professional duty and personal responsibility, and encourages discussion on whether healthcare should be conditional.
Should companies be required to disclose their use of AI in hiring decisions?	This explores the competing values of transparency, privacy and business interests, and asks whether job applicants have a right to know how decisions about them are being made, leading to arguments on both sides.

As you can see, a descriptive approach is not appropriate for your reflective project. Instead, you need to take an interrogative approach. Your project should challenge you to:

- think critically about complex issues with no simple answers
- reflect on your own values and how they influence your thinking
- develop and present arguments using evidence and reasoning.

To make sure that you are on the right track with your research question, check that it will lead to debate. If the answer is very one-sided, it is probably descriptive and should be revised. For example:

- Ethical issue: Child labour in global supply chains
- Descriptive question: 'What is child labour and where does it occur?'
- Interrogative question: 'Knowing that many low-income communities rely on revenue from all family members, should child labour be entirely illegal?'

You should also look for value conflicts – for example, does your question involve competing principles such as safety vs freedom, individual rights vs community needs or profit vs environmental impact? These things indicate that your approach is sufficiently interrogative.

Overlooking the ethical dilemma

Be careful of choosing a topic that might generate a heated debate, but which lacks a genuine ethical conflict between moral principles. Controversial topics are issues that people argue about, often based on facts, preferences or political positions. These are not always the same as ethical dilemmas, which involve conflicts between moral principles where both sides have legitimate ethical concerns.

Examples of topics *without* an ethical dilemma

Topic	Explanation
Which is better: Android or iPhone?	This is about product features and personal preferences.
Is climate change caused by human activity?	This is a scientific question with a factual answer, not a conflict of moral principles.
Would the introduction of video refereeing improve the modern game of football?	This is an open question that would encourage different points of view and would lead to a good discussion and debate, but it does not involve an ethical dilemma.

Examples of topics *with* an ethical dilemma

Topic	Explanation
Should low-income countries be required to limit their economic growth to address climate change, even if it means reduced living standards for their citizens?	This is an ethical dilemma related to climate change reflecting the tension between collective responsibility for preventing climate catastrophe against distributive justice and lower income countries' rights to pursue economic prosperity.
Is big data analysis a conflict of interest with consumer privacy?	This is an ethical dilemma related to technology reflecting the tension between utilitarian benefits of data analysis for societal greater good against individual autonomy and the fundamental right to privacy.
Should schools be permitted to monitor student's online activity to prevent cyberbullying, even if it violates student privacy?	This is an ethical dilemma related to education reflecting the tension between schools' duty of care to protect students from harm against respect for student autonomy and privacy rights.

There are several ways to check that your topic contains an ethical dilemma:

The debate test	The value test	The complexity test	The ethics test
Would this question generate debate?	What moral principles or values are in conflict in this question?	Are there good reasons to support differing opinions and positions?	Does this question involve what people should do (ethics) rather than what they could do (facts/capabilities)?

Identifying an ethical dilemma and developing a research question

The first step is to identify an ethical dilemma and create a research question linked to your career interest. Using the funnel approach helps narrow your focus, deepen your understanding of the ethical complexity, and choose a dilemma that interests and motivates you throughout the project.

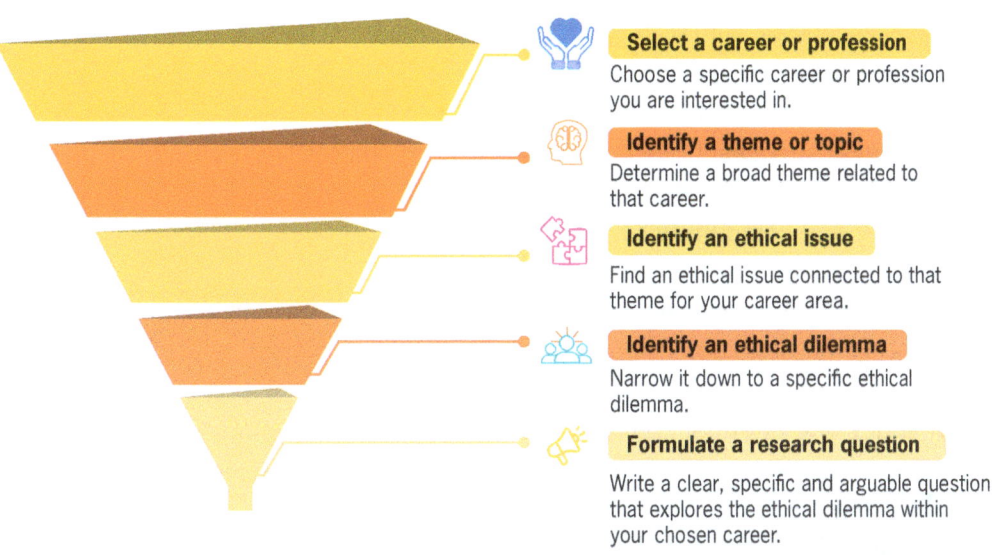

The funnel approach

Select a career or profession
Choose a specific career or profession you are interested in.

Identify a theme or topic
Determine a broad theme related to that career.

Identify an ethical issue
Find an ethical issue connected to that theme for your career area.

Identify an ethical dilemma
Narrow it down to a specific ethical dilemma.

Formulate a research question
Write a clear, specific and arguable question that explores the ethical dilemma within your chosen career.

Step 1: Choose a specific career or profession you are interested in

Your choice of career or profession could be related to your career-related studies, but it could also emerge from a subject of interest from your Diploma Programme courses, or it could be one of your future career aspirations. The key is to ensure that it has real-world relevance and is from an area that genuinely connects with your interests or passions. You might consider some of the following areas: business and finance; healthcare and medicine; arts and design; technology and IT; journalism and media; performing arts; law and legal services; social work and community services; education; aeronautics and aviation; environmental science; sports management and coaching.

> **Remember**
>
> Remember – you will be working with this topic for an extended period, so it is important that it continues to motivate and intrigue you.

Step 2: Identify a theme or topic

You next need to decide on a broad theme or topic related to the career you have selected. Start broadly by exploring the general areas of professional practice, common workplace situations or key responsibilities that professionals in your area of interest encounter. Here are some examples of broad themes or topics related to different career fields:

 Business and finance: Corporate governance, consumer relations, workplace practices, financial reporting, supply chain management, marketing and advertising, automation and innovation.

 Healthcare and medicine: Patient care, medical research and innovation, resource allocation, professional relationships, end-of-life care, public health initiatives.

 Arts and design: Creative expression, cultural representation, artistic authenticity, production practices, audience engagement, intellectual property, digitisation of art, the value of art.

 Technology and IT: Data management, software development, user experience, digital innovation, cybersecurity, artificial intelligence applications.

 Journalism and media: News reporting, source protection, editorial decision-making, media representation, digital journalism, investigative reporting.

 Performing arts: Performance standards, industry relationships, casting process, creative collaboration, audience interaction, career development, artistic integrity.

 Law and legal services: Client representation, court proceedings, legal advice, professional conduct, access to justice, legal system reform.

 Social work and community services: Client support, resource distribution, community intervention, professional boundaries, advocacy work, policy implementation.

 Education: Student development, curriculum design and implementation, classroom management, assessment practices, education opportunities, institutional policies, education reform, teacher training.

 Aeronautics and aviation: Flight operations, safety protocols, environmental considerations, technological advancement, industry regulation, crisis management, airport locations and constructions.

 Environmental science: Conservation efforts, research methodology, policy development, community engagement, sustainable practices, urban planning, environmental monitoring.

 Sports management and coaching: Athlete development, competitive practices, team management, performance optimisation, industry governance, community engagement, sporting events management, sports psychology.

Learning journal entry

Activity

Create a mind map to explore different facets of your career interest. Write your career interest in the middle, then branch out with different themes or topics you have heard about or discovered. For each theme or topic, consider what general areas or professional practice it involves. Which themes or topics make you most curious to learn more and why?

Step 3: Identify an ethical issue

After choosing a broad theme, identify a specific ethical issue within it. Move from general career areas to situations where values or stakeholder interests conflict. To help you brainstorm, here are examples from different fields:

 Business and finance: Ethical sourcing, fair trade, data privacy, marketing ethics, corporate social responsibility versus profit maximisation, transparency in reporting financial information, and balancing shareholder interests with employee welfare.

 Healthcare and medicine: Patient autonomy versus family wishes, end-of-life decision-making, maintaining patient confidentiality while protecting others from harm, resource allocation with limited supplies, medical research ethics, genetic engineering, balancing individual care with public health needs.

 Arts and design: Inspiration versus plagiarism, cultural appropriation versus appreciation, controversial art, authenticity versus provenance in art, fair labour and production, sustainability and environmental impact.

 Technology and IT: Data privacy versus innovation, accessibility of technology across socioeconomic groups, responsibility for how software is used by others, the ethical use of AI, data security, algorithmic bias, social media impact, intellectual property rights, and balancing automation benefits with employment impacts.

 Journalism and media: Protecting sources versus public interest, privacy of individuals versus news value, objectivity versus advocacy, speed of reporting versus accuracy verification, and editorial independence versus commercial pressures.

 Performing arts: Presentation and authenticity, power dynamics and abuse, intellectual property and rights, audience engagement and consent, physical and mental health of performers, casting procedure and process.

 Law and legal services: Justice versus legality, prosecutorial discretion, client confidentiality versus preventing harm to others, human rights, conflicts of interest in representation, personal beliefs versus professional obligation, and access to justice versus financial viability.

 Social work and community services: Client autonomy versus protection from harm, confidentiality versus mandatory reporting requirements, fair distribution of limited resources among clients, professional boundaries in close relationships, and individual advocacy versus *systemic* change.

 Education: Academic integrity, inclusive practices, student privacy, teacher-student relationships, curriculum development and accessibility.

 Aeronautics and aviation: Safety and reliability, environmental impact, intellectual property and data security, fairness and discrimination, crisis management and communication, airport location versus environmental responsibility.

 Environmental science: Sustainable development, conservation versus economic growth, pollution control, resource depletion, short-term human needs versus long-term environmental sustainability, local community interests versus global environmental concerns, and scientific objectivity versus advocacy for environmental causes.

 Sports management and coaching: Athlete wellbeing versus performance demands, fair play and sportspersonship, power dynamics and abuse, coaching conduct and role modelling, financial ethics and transparency, athlete exploitation and welfare, fair competition and integrity, social responsibility and inclusivity.

Learning journal entry

Reflection

Which ethical issues in your career field of interest surprised you the most? What made them surprising?

Having identified an ethical issue, try to formulate a question that asks you to describe what you know about the issue. This will set the stage for deeper inquiry.

Example

Formulating a question

Here are some examples of how to turn an issue into an initial question.

- If your issue is child labour, your initial question might be: 'How does child labour affect both the children and the economy in a country, and what is being done to prevent it?'
- If your issue is patient confidentiality, you might explore scenarios such as: 'What legal steps must a doctor follow when patient confidentiality conflicts with protecting others from harm?'
- If your issue is data privacy, you might ask: 'What measures should companies implement to protect user data while maintaining business growth?'

Step 4: Identify an ethical dilemma

Narrow down the ethical issue to a specific ethical dilemma – a situation where there are conflicting values or courses of action and no clear 'right' answer. Refine your initial question so that it asks for one solution to the problem or issue, then transform it so that it leads to multiple answers and perspectives.

Example

Refining your question

Here are some examples of how to focus an ethical issue on a specific dilemma:

Issue	Initial question	Refined question
Child labour	'How does child labour affect both the children and the economy in a country, and what is being done to prevent it?'	'Knowing that many poor communities rely on income from all family members, should child labour be entirely illegal?'
Patient confidentiality	'What legal steps must a doctor follow when patient confidentiality conflicts with protecting others from harm?'	'Should healthcare professionals breach patient confidentiality when it conflicts with their duty to protect others from harm?'
Data privacy	'What measures should companies implement to protect user data while maintaining business growth?'	'Should companies prioritise protecting user data over technological innovation and business growth?'

> **Remember**
>
> When it comes to ethical dilemmas, people may disagree about what is right because different values conflict with each other. These competing values, principles or potential outcomes make the decision complex. Your question should invite discussion and exploration of different perspectives.

> **Learning journal entry**
>
> **Activity**
>
> Write about a time when you had to make a difficult decision. How did you decide what to do? What values guided your choice?
>
> **Reflection**
>
> Think about the dilemma you have identified. What personal experiences or values make you care about this issue? How might someone from a different background see it differently?

Step 5: Formulate a research question

Write a clear, specific and arguable question that explores the ethical dilemma within your chosen career field. Your final research question should be:

- clear and specific – it should identify an ethical dilemma and clearly connect it to a career or profession
- focused – it should be narrow enough to explore in depth within the scope of your project, targeting a specific aspect of the dilemma such as a particular group, setting or situation rather than trying to address every possible angle; avoid a question that is too broad (which would make it unmanageable), or too narrow (which would limit analysis)
- open to multiple solutions – your question should invite analysis and discussion from different perspectives and contexts, allowing for more than one possible answer or approach and complex ethical reasoning.

For example:

Unfocused question	Focused question
How does medical ethics affect healthcare?	To what extent should doctors breach patient confidentiality to protect third parties from harm in emergency situations?

> **Remember**
>
> Your question should make some people think: 'That's a good question – I can see arguments on both sides.'
>
> You should also avoid questions that begin with 'What', 'Why', 'How', 'Who', 'Where' or 'When'. These lead to explanations and descriptive answers, rather than debates.
>
> Instead, use starters such as:
>
> - 'Should'
> - 'Should ... even if'

- 'Is it appropriate …'
- 'Can … be justified …'
- 'To what extent is … ethically justifiable?'
- 'Is it ethical to…'

Decision-making checklist

As you brainstorm and refine your ideas, ask yourself these questions to help you decide on the best ethical dilemma for your project.

Interest and engagement
- ✓ Does this dilemma genuinely intrigue me?
- ✓ Can I see myself staying engaged with this topic for 10 months or longer?
- ✓ Does it connect to my personal values or experiences in meaningful ways?

Complexity and depth
- ✓ Are there at least two clearly conflicting ethical principles or values?
- ✓ Does the dilemma resist simple 'right' or 'wrong' answers?
- ✓ Are there multiple stakeholders with legitimate but competing interests?

Research potential
- ✓ Can I find multiple perspectives on this dilemma in academic sources, professional journals, case studies or real-world examples?
- ✓ Are there current debates or ongoing discussions about this issue?
- ✓ Is there sufficient material available to support a thorough investigation?

Career relevance
- ✓ Is this a dilemma I might realistically encounter in my future profession?
- ✓ Does addressing this dilemma help me develop skills or knowledge relevant to my future career?
- ✓ Would understanding this dilemma better prepare me for professional practice in the future?

Personal growth potential
- ✓ Will exploring this dilemma challenge my thinking or broaden my perspective?
- ✓ Does it require me to consider viewpoints different from my own?
- ✓ Will it help me develop my ethical thinking and reasoning skills?

Test your top choices

Before making your final selection, test your top two or three choices by carrying out some brief preliminary research. Spend some time exploring each dilemma online, looking for:

- recent news articles or case studies
- professional association guidelines or statements
- academic articles or ethical analyses
- different stakeholder perspectives.

This initial research will help you decide whether enough material exists and whether the dilemma maintains your interest when you delve deeper.

> **Remember**
>
> Document this process in your learning journal to connect it to your learning journey. Record your initial brainstorming, your evaluation of different options and your reasoning for your final choice. This will become valuable for understanding your own ethical development and decision-making process.
>
> Also, look back at your journal entries from previous chapters. How might the ethical dilemma you are considering connect to your earlier reflections on career interests, values and goals? This review will ensure your project feels integrated and personally meaningful rather than just an academic exercise.

Below are a few examples from learners that show how to take your initial thoughts or ethical dilemmas and turn them into well-crafted research questions. They use the funnel approach, along with the key tips provided earlier.

> **Example**
>
> **The entertainment industry and #MeToo**
>
> Athena is an aspiring performing artist focused on music theatre and performing arts. After some initial research, she became interested in how policies in the entertainment industry have evolved since the #MeToo movement.
>
> | Career/profession | Entertainment industry |
> |---|---|
> | Theme | Social justice |
> | Ethical issue | Misconduct, power dynamics, harassment |
> | Ethical dilemma | Balancing the need to address misconduct allegations with the rights of the accused. |
> | Research question | Given the effects the #MeToo movement has had on the entertainment industry, should a policy be made to ban people with misconduct records from working in the industry?

Or

Should casting professionals exclude actors based on unresolved misconduct allegations without legal verdicts? |
>
> Using the funnel approach, Athena refined and created a research question that she felt met all the criteria and would serve as a solid foundation for her project:
>
> > 'Given the effects the #MeToo movement has had on the entertainment industry, should casting professionals exclude actors based on unresolved misconduct allegations without legal verdicts?'
>
> This presents a challenging ethical dilemma that resonates with recent discussions in the entertainment field, prompting consideration of the tension between addressing misconduct and upholding the accused actors' career and individual rights. This question also puts Athena in the shoes of future professionals in the entertainment industry, asking her to think about the difficult decisions casting directors and other industry leaders must make. It encourages her to consider what values and responsibilities are most important in these situations, and to explore the real-life consequences of different choices for all those involved.

Example

The culinary arts and sugar content in confectionary products

Patrick studies culinary arts and is interested in the food industry. As a child, he ate a lot of sugary foods, which caused health problems. Because of this experience, he wanted to explore ethical issues related to the amount of sugar in sweets.

Career/profession	Culinary arts/food manufacturing
Theme	Public health
Ethical issue	Public health concerns related to excessive sugar consumption
Ethical dilemma	Balancing consumer appeal and profitability with the health impacts of high sugar content.
Research question	Should confectionery manufacturers prioritise reducing sugar content in their products over maintaining consumer appeal and profitability? Or Should the government regulate the amount of sugar allowed in confectionary products?

Using the funnel method, Patrick initially framed his research question as: 'Should confectionery manufacturers prioritise reducing sugar content in their products over maintaining consumer appeal and profitability?' He felt this question allowed for a nuanced analysis of his future career dilemma and multiple perspectives. However, after reading an article about government policies on sugar intake in confectionery products in Japan, he shifted his focus. He revised his research question to:

'Should the government regulate the amount of sugar used in confectionary products?'

This new question connects to broader societal debates about government roles, corporate responsibility, and public health. He recognised that government regulation could have significant implications for the confectionary industry, consumers, and public health authorities, placing the future practitioner in a more impactful role where ethical considerations could lead to wide-ranging consequences.

Remember

You have complete control over your project, and it is important to identify an ethical dilemma that you feel strongly about. Think of yourself as a future practitioner – your research question should not only be meaningful; it should also be relevant to the kinds of ethical decisions you might face in your career.

Learning journal entry

Reflection

Choosing your ethical dilemma and research question:

- What ethical dilemma have you identified and what drew you to this dilemma?
- How does it connect to your earlier journal entries about your career interests and values?

- What steps have you taken to refine your research question? Does it clearly capture the ethical dilemma you wish to explore?
- What aspect of this dilemma do you think will challenge your current thinking?
- What do you hope to learn about yourself and your future career through exploring this dilemma?

Reflection on feedback

What feedback have you received from your peers and/or supervisor about your research question? What are your action plans for addressing this feedback?

Activity

What challenges do you anticipate in exploring your ethical dilemma? Write a brief plan explaining how you will overcome or manage them.

Choosing your project format

Once you have laid the groundwork by identifying an ethical dilemma and working up a suitable research question, your next important decision is how you are going to present your reflective project. There are many different formats you could choose from: written, audio, visual or multimedia. The diagram below shows just a few examples of the formats available to you.

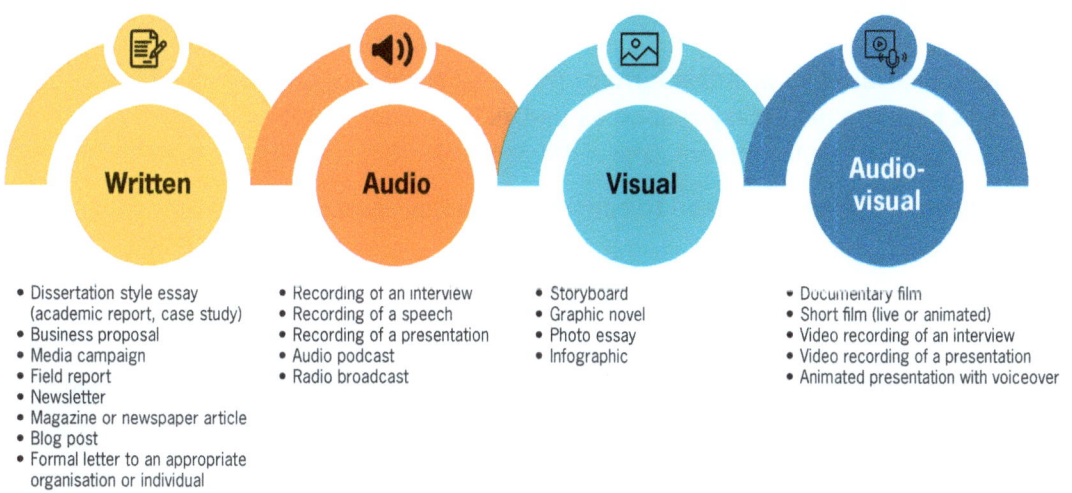

Written
- Dissertation style essay (academic report, case study)
- Business proposal
- Media campaign
- Field report
- Newsletter
- Magazine or newspaper article
- Blog post
- Formal letter to an appropriate organisation or individual

Audio
- Recording of an interview
- Recording of a speech
- Recording of a presentation
- Audio podcast
- Radio broadcast

Visual
- Storyboard
- Graphic novel
- Photo essay
- Infographic

Audio-visual
- Documentary film
- Short film (live or animated)
- Video recording of an interview
- Video recording of a presentation
- Animated presentation with voiceover

Remember

Your final project must stay within a 4,000-word limit, which includes a reflection statement of up to 1,000 words on the final reflection form (FRF). No matter which format you choose, the same assessment criteria apply.

When choosing a format, consider:
- which **communication** styles you are familiar with and enjoy
- which suits your skills and personal preferences
- what types of projects are common in your chosen career field.

The reflective project offers a unique opportunity to create something that mirrors authentic professional outputs. Ask yourself, 'How would a professional in my chosen field share their ideas or communicate?'

For example:

- If you are aiming for a career in the film and television industry, consider creating a film or documentary to present your research and analysis.
- If you are pursuing arts and design, a photo essay, storyboard or narrated presentation with visuals might be the way to go.
- For those interested in game design, producing an animation or audio-visual project could be ideal.
- If your ambition lies in business and marketing, a business proposal, or media campaign might be the right fit.

Sometimes, the specific nature of your chosen ethical dilemma can guide your format choice. For example, if you plan to discuss the ethical dilemma surrounding mature topics in children's television shows, analysing popular children's television shows might be more effective through a film or video product rather than a written description. Similarly, if your topic involves copyright issues in music production, using audio clips could be more impactful than complex written jargon to describe chord progression.

Below are some questions to consider for each format option.

- **Why does this format suit your project?** Consider why this format fits *your* ethical dilemma, *your* career interests and how *you* want to present your ideas.
- **How does this format link to your career area?** Reflect on how professionals in your chosen field typically communicate their ideas or research.
- **How effective will this format be for conveying your ideas?** Consider how well this format allows you to explore and present the ethical dilemma and your personal position.
- **How familiar are you with this format?** Be honest about your experience and comfort level.
- **Do you have the necessary resources and skills to complete this format successfully?** Think about equipment, software, time and support.

Are there any other factors you need to consider? For example, accessibility, audience preferences or project constraints.

Example

Here is how Gentle reflected on the choice of a film for her reflective project research question: 'Should television shows aimed towards children (from ages 4–7) discuss mature topics (such as violence, current affairs or discrimination)?'

There were three main reasons why I chose to do a film over a written essay format.

Firstly, I found it easier to organise the two separate components (the film and the final written reflection) that were being examined. Each section can be fully focused on presenting and reflecting on the research I've done, respectively. I could fully flesh out my research and conclusions uninterrupted, and I could focus on reflecting because the written portion did not need to serve the dual purpose of reinforcing the information from the video.

Secondly, with TV being a visual medium, it was easier to show clips than to waste my word count on describing each study in depth. It also allowed me to feature many more examples that I'd found in my research but couldn't fit into my script.

Lastly, I like films and knew I would enjoy the process. I watch them in my spare time, editing videos is one of my hobbies, and I felt less stressed about writing in the semi-formal tone of a film compared to an academic written essay. Since I knew that the final product was in a format I was comfortable with making, I could focus my attention on the contents of my Reflective Project rather than the output.

Learning journal entry

Activity

Choose the two format options that most appeal to you or that you think are most appropriate for your chosen field. Note down answers to the questions above for each format, then compare them to decide which one best fits your project and personal strengths.

Reflection

Reflect on your choice:

- What is one strength and one potential challenge you expect to face with this format?
- How will you prepare to overcome this challenge?
- Who can you ask for help or advice if you encounter difficulties with this format?

The common goal across all reflective project formats is to present information about an identified ethical dilemma, explore how it is perceived by different stakeholders and communities in varying contexts, and articulate your personal position. Regardless of format, ensure you use appropriate terminology, **structural elements**, and conventions of style for your chosen format. Make sure your project targets your intended audience group or organisation, as you would in a speech, presentation, formal letter or a general essay to a general audience.

You can find more information and activities to help you create a successful format for your reflective project in Chapter 7.

Identifying and understanding differing perspectives and contexts

To develop a comprehensive project, you must consider how different people and communities view – and are affected by – your ethical dilemma. Understanding these different perspectives and contexts is crucial because it:

- prevents you from seeing only one side
- helps you understand why people disagree with each other
- shows how location, culture and circumstances affect ethical decisions
- demonstrates that ethical dilemmas are complex and interconnected.

Understanding perspectives

Perspective is the 'lens' through which different people see the world, shaped by their own background, personal experiences, values and beliefs. Like viewing a sculpture from different angles, examining an ethical dilemma from different perspectives reveals new details and insights. For example, when making decisions about end-of-life care, different stakeholders may approach the same situation with varying priorities:

- A doctor may focus on medical ethics and professional guidelines.
- A patient may value personal autonomy and quality of life.
- A family member may prioritise emotional wellbeing and cultural or religious beliefs.
- An insurance company may consider cost-effectiveness and policy coverage.

When considering different perspectives, it is important to avoid slipping into stereotypes or making assumptions about how different groups think or behave. Real people's views are shaped by their history, culture, religion and individual experiences.

So, in the example above you would need to remember that:

- not all healthcare professionals will prioritise the same ethical principles
- patients' preferences are shaped by complex personal, cultural and religious factors
- family members may have diverse views even within the same family
- organisations like insurance companies may have varied policies and approaches.

> **Remember**
>
> Instead of assuming what a group thinks, explore what different individuals within that group might value or prioritise. This is especially important when considering marginalised communities or cultural groups – always seek authentic voices and diverse sources rather than making generalisations.

Understanding contexts

Context is made up of the circumstances, events and settings that influence how an issue is understood and experienced. Context helps explain why the same ethical dilemma might be viewed differently in different places or times.

There are two main types of contexts relevant for your reflective project: **local context** and **global context.**

Local context includes the specific characteristics of a place or community, including:

- cultural traditions and values
- economic conditions
- political systems
- geographic factors
- historical events
- environmental factors
- local policies, rules and regulations.

Global context considers the bigger picture – what is happening around the world, how different places and people are connected, and the shared challenges that all humans face, including:

- international trends and movements
- global economic systems
- worldwide challenges such as climate change or pandemics
- international laws and agreements.

Some of the local contexts such as political systems, geographic factors, historical events, economic and environmental factors can also be applied to global contexts.

Contextualisation means looking at something within its surroundings to better understand why it happens or exists in a certain way. When you analyse an ethical dilemma for your reflective project, it is essential to look at the different contexts in which the dilemma occurs. This will help you fully understand the dilemma and its effects.

> **Remember**
>
> When examining local contexts, consider how the same ethical dilemma might be experienced differently in various local communities around the world. For example, examine the local factors in your immediate community alongside the local factors in a different or distant community elsewhere in the world. This comparative approach helps you understand how the same ethical dilemma can be experienced very differently depending on local circumstances.

Connecting ethical dilemmas with perspectives and contexts

An ethical dilemma can affect individuals, groups, local and global communities, so it is important to consider the perspectives of different stakeholders and how the dilemma is viewed in context. Analysing it from multiple perspectives, including cultural, social, historical and economic factors, deepens your understanding and shows how people and communities are interconnected. A good starting point is to identify the key stakeholders involved. You can then use the research tools in Chapter 5 to explore relevant contexts, such as historical background, traditions, societal trends, ideologies, ethical principles and political or economic systems.

> **Remember**
>
> In the assessment criteria, perspectives are linked to Criterion A, while contexts relate to criteria A and B (which focuses on the impact of the dilemma). Additionally, Criterion C requires you to critically analyse these perspectives and synthesise them into a coherent understanding that informs your personal position.

Mapping stakeholders and perspectives

Step 1: Identify your stakeholders

List all the people or groups affected by your ethical dilemma. Think broadly:

- Who makes decisions about this issue?
- Who is directly affected by those decisions?
- Who pays the costs or receives the benefits?
- Who has the power to change things?
- Who has no power but is still affected?

Step 2: Understand each perspective

For each stakeholder, ask:

- What are their main concerns about this dilemma?
- What values or principles guide their thinking and decision-making?
- What do they have to gain or lose?
- What constraints or pressures do they face?

Step 3: Explore different contexts

Research how your dilemma plays out:

- in different countries or cultures
- in different socioeconomic (poor versus wealthy) communities
- in urban versus rural settings
- in different historical periods
- under different social and political systems

> **Example**
>
> Remember Patrick, who was examining the ethical dilemma of balancing consumer appeal and profitability with the health impacts of high sugar content in confectionary products? His research question was: 'Should the government regulate the amount of sugar allowed in confectionary products?'
>
> The stakeholders here would be consumers, manufacturers, health organisations and government agencies. To explore different perspectives, Patrick might ask:
>
> - How do consumers view sugar in confectionary, and what do they expect regarding health and taste?
> - What are the economic effects on manufacturers if sugar content is regulated?
> - How do health organisations view the impact of high sugar intake on public health, and what evidence do they have?

- What political considerations do governments face in regulating sugar, and how might this affect their relationship with the food industry? Can I find examples where government intervention in the food industry – or in similar industries – has had positive or negative effects?
- How do governments balance their responsibilities to protect the health and wellbeing of citizens with the interests of businesses and consumers?

Patrick could explore the different contexts by looking at things like cultural attitudes towards sweets, historical trends in sugar consumption, societal shifts in health awareness and economic systems affecting food production and regulation. These will help him understand the ethical complexities of regulating sugar content in confectionary products. It is also important to note that policies and practices related to sugar regulation can differ significantly across regions, countries, and cultures. Here, Patrick could compare the different policies between Japan and other countries or regions.

Learning journal entry

Activity

Make notes on the following questions:

- Who are the key stakeholders involved in your chosen ethical dilemma?
- What different perspectives can you identify regarding your chosen ethical dilemma?
- What local factors – such as geography, culture, economy, environment and politics – influence the ethical dilemma in the specific community or place you are in?
- Choose a different community elsewhere in the world that faces the same ethical dilemma. How might the local factors (geography, culture, economy, environment, politics) differ in that community, and what impact might these differences have on how the ethical dilemma is experienced and addressed?
- How do broader global contexts such as international social trends, global political events or movements, environmental challenges, or worldwide economic systems, affect or connect to your understanding of the ethical dilemma?

Now draft a Reflective Project proposal with an outline of your research question, project objective, rationale, research plan, your intended format option, and personalised timeline.

Reflection

Reflect on what you have discovered:

- Has anything surprised or challenged you in these early explorations of your ethical dilemma?
- In what ways do you think your own background or experiences influence how you currently view this dilemma?
- How do you think the perspectives of others, especially those from different cultures or backgrounds, might shape their views on this dilemma?
- What have you learned about the ethical principles involved, and how has this affected your thinking about the dilemma?

Feedback

What questions do you still have about your reflective project plan? Did you receive any feedback from your supervisor and/or peers about your plan? Record the feedback you have received in your learning journal and outline an action plan to address how you would like to act on the feedback.

Key takeaways: Chapter 4

- There are two common issues with the reflective project that you should be aware of and need to avoid.
- Choose an ethical dilemma that matters to you and connects to your future career aspiration. This will keep you motivated and make your project more meaningful.
- Turn your dilemma into a clear, focused research question. A strong question guides your research and helps you explore different perspectives and possible solutions.
- Consider various formats for your project, including written, audio, visual and audio-visual options. Select a format that aligns with your skills, preferences and the expectations of your future career field. Remember, the format should help you clearly present your ideas and communicate your research findings.
- Recognise that ethical dilemmas are influenced by diverse perspectives and contexts. Understand the local and global factors that shape these dilemmas. This will deepen your understanding and show the complexity of your ethical dilemma.

Key terms

contextualisation: placing an idea within its relevant background or framework, showing how it fits into the larger picture

global context: the big picture of what is happening around the world; how different places and people are connected and the common issues or challenges that affect many countries and communities

intercultural understanding: the ability to recognise and respect cultural differences and interact effectively with people from different cultural backgrounds

local context: the specific features and conditions of a particular place or community, such as its geography, culture, economy, environment and politics

methodology: the research approaches, frameworks, and strategies used in a particular discipline

structural elements: the features that characterise how a piece of writing or other presentation format is organised, such as formatting, chapter headings, titles and subtitles, page breaks, dialogue tagging, grammar, punctuation, spelling, capitalisation, paragraphing and citation styles

systemic: relating to things that are about or affect a whole system

Chapter 5 – The research and analysis phase: Research

This chapter covers the following:
- The importance of research and analysis
- Conducting research
- Types of research
- Finding and evaluating sources
- Citing sources
- Understanding ethical research in the reflective project and using AI

Learner profile traits

knowledgeable

thinkers

principled

The importance of research and analysis

The research and analysis phase is an important part of your reflective project learning journey, involving several higher-level **thinking** skills. This chapter will guide you through these skills and the process of research and analysis in a logical way.

First you will explore why research is essential for your reflective project and be guided through the practical steps of conducting ethical, effective research. You will learn how to gather information using appropriate methods, evaluate sources critically, cite properly and use AI responsibly.

In the following chapter, you will then build on this foundation, learning how to organise, analyse and synthesise your research findings to develop your personal position. You will explore some of the analytical tools and frameworks that can help you make sense of complex ethical dilemmas and form well-reasoned conclusions.

Conducting research

Research is all about gathering, evaluating and using information effectively. For your reflective project, you will need to manage your research carefully and respect academic integrity, including using technology in an ethical way.

Research is very important; it links to three of the five reflective project assessment criteria:

- Criterion A looks at how clearly you explain your ethical dilemma and explore different perspectives. Both require thorough research.
- Criterion B focuses on the depth and breadth of your research, including the variety of resources you use and the **knowledge** gained through the process.
- Criterion C highlights how research helps you create well-informed, evidence-based arguments and responses to your ethical dilemma.

As you can see, research plays a critical role, encouraging you to investigate your ethical dilemma thoroughly, consider multiple viewpoints, and develop a well-supported personal stance based on your findings.

> **Remember**
>
> The reflective project learning journey and the research process are not always straightforward. Just like projects you will encounter in your future profession, they can get messy! In this book, the process is split into distinct phases; however, these stages will sometimes overlap. You might need to go back to earlier steps as you discover new information, make new connections during your analysis phase, or receive feedback from your supervisor and mentors. Research is an evolving process!

Types of research

Research methods are the tools and techniques you use to collect data or evidence for your project. There are two main types, each serving a different purpose and providing a different type of information.

- **Primary research** involves collecting original data directly to answer specific questions related to your research. Methods include **surveys** and questionnaires, interviews, focus groups, observations, experiments and case studies.
- **Secondary research** involves analysing existing data, which has been collected by others, often to provide background information before conducting primary research. Methods include literature reviews, government reports, books, academic journals, online databases and news articles.

There are advantages and disadvantages to each type of research.

Research type	Advantages	Disadvantages
Primary research	- Specificity: Tailored to your specific needs. - Up-to-date information: Provides current data (first-hand). - Unique insights: Uncovers new insights that secondary research may not provide. - Control: You have authority over the data collection process. - In-depth insights: Allows deeper exploration.	- Time-consuming: Collecting data from scratch takes considerable time and effort. - Limited sample size: Often represents a small population. - Potential **bias**: Risk of unintentional bias in data collection. - Limited scope: May not cover a wide range of information. - Not self-dependent: Relies on participants' availability.
Secondary research	- Time-saving: Quickly gather information from existing sources. - Broader scope: Covers larger populations and historical trends. - Accessibility: Sources are readily available. - Self-dependent: Does not rely on participants' availability. - Opportunity for further research: Identifies gaps in existing knowledge and research.	- Outdated information: Data may not be current. - Lack of specificity: May not align perfectly with your needs. - Quality issues: Source reliability can vary. - Limited ability: Cannot explore specific questions deeply. - Limited control: You cannot influence how the data was collected.

You can also use a **mixed approach**, combining both primary and secondary sources for a more comprehensive view of your research question.

Choosing your research methods

Choose the research method(s) that fit your project goals, available resources and the context of your study. Look at examples of completed reflective projects to see what others have done and how they chose their methods based on their topic and format. Think practically: How much time do you have? What resources or tools do you need? Do you have the skills to carry out your chosen methods?

Start by checking existing primary sources, as these often have high-quality information and can save time. Here are some examples of primary data sources – but note that, depending on how you use these, some might be considered secondary sources:

- video/podcast interviews
- autobiographies and letters
- speeches and lectures
- experiment results
- original documents (laws, policies, and so on)
- case studies
- company reports and statistics
- blog posts, social media and online forum discussions – please make sure you check for bias before deciding to use them.

However, you may find that it makes sense to do your own primary research, especially if you want to:

- obtain specific information from experts
- compare information from other communities to your local context
- address niche topics with limited published data.

> **Remember**
>
> While each method has strengths and limitations, combining primary and secondary sources usually gives you a fuller understanding of your topic. Secondary research can provide background information and historical context, while primary research fills gaps and offers first-hand insights.

Research methodology: your research roadmap

Research methodology is the big-picture plan that guides how you carry out your research. It includes the different methods, techniques and approaches you will use to gather, analyse and understand your data in an organised way. Think of your methodology as your roadmap – it shows how you plan to carry out your research while keeping in mind any challenges or limitations you might face. While methods are the 'how' of research, methodology answers the 'why' – why you choose certain methods based on your research question and goals. Choosing the right research methodology is critical because it shapes your whole project. A well-designed methodology helps you select the best methods and makes sure your findings are valid and reliable.

The following table explains some of the key components of research methodology.

Key component	What it means
Research design	Your overall plan for how you will conduct your research.
Data collection methods	How you plan to collect your data – will you use primary research, secondary research, or both?
Data analysis techniques	How you will analyse your data and draw conclusions.
Ethical considerations	The rules and **principles** you need to follow to conduct your research responsibly and respectfully.
Validity and reliability	How will you ensure the accuracy and trustworthiness of your data?
Bias and limitations	Potential limitations of your research design and biases that may influence your interpretation of results.

Managing your research

- ✓ Prioritise your tasks: Focus on the most important sources first.
- ✓ Set clear goals: Break down your research into manageable chunks.
- ✓ Create a schedule: Allocate specific time blocks for different research activities.

   > For example, after conducting a general literary review, you can start to schedule activities and events such as finding more case studies or designing surveys to gather primary data.

- ✓ Take breaks: Regular breaks prevent burnout and maintain productivity.

The following examples show the ways in which varying research methodologies were used to successful effect based on the nature of the research topic and available resources.

Example

Student A: Casey

Ethical dilemma: Artists' creative freedom vs sustainable art creation

Research question: 'Should artists prioritise environmental sustainability over creative freedom when selecting materials and mediums?'

'To explore this dilemma, I used both primary and secondary sources. An interview was used as a main source of primary data to gain different perspectives, where student and professional artists were both sub-divided into sustainable artists (those who use eco-friendly materials like recycled substances, natural pigments and biodegradable components to minimise environmental harm) and unsustainable artists<1> (those who primarily use traditional materials containing toxic chemicals, synthetic substances and non-biodegradable materials that contribute to pollution and resource depletion).

There were 16 professional artists, nine student artists and five sustainable artists. I interviewed different types of artists, from painters to sculptors, to explore how the different media affects the artist's perspective<2>. The questionnaire contained six or seven questions, depending on the quality of their answers. The questions were used to understand their thought process to acquire a common limitation among artists. For sustainable artists specifically, I explored the extent to which their art is sustainable by asking questions on what happens to the artwork if it was not sold.

In addition, I personally attempted to make sustainable art to explore the dilemma further and explore multiple perspectives<3>. I started by initiating a sustainable crafts workshop to educate young learners on sustainability. Then I also attempted to make sustainable art and reflected on my experiences and challenges.

For my secondary data I used a variety of databases, such as online websites, pdf journals and books. I analysed artworks from the book *Raw Materials* to explore what is perceived as sustainable from both society and the artist's perspective. I also used websites and online journals to gain a better understanding of the history of sustainability and sustainable art<4>. Moreover, journals were beneficial to learn the multiple perspectives on sustainable art.'

Commentary: Casey's hands-on experimental approach pairs comprehensive interviews and personal art creation (primary) with extensive secondary research through databases, journals and books to understand both historical context and current perspectives on sustainable art, giving her project authentic depth and theoretical grounding.

<1> Strategic bias mitigation: Casey deliberately structured her sample to include contrasting perspectives (sustainable vs unsustainable artists) to capture multiple viewpoints rather than confirming a single perspective. This reflects methodological triangulation through diverse participant selection.

<2> Perspective diversification: By including artists working in different media, Casey actively sought to understand whether her findings were consistent across different art forms, or if medium-specific factors influenced views on sustainability.

<3> Practice-based research integration: Casey employed a practice-based research approach by positioning herself as both researcher and experimental subject. This self-experimentation method gave her 'insider knowledge' of the practical constraints and creative challenges of using sustainable materials, providing direct experiential data that could not be accessed through interviews alone. As a researcher-practitioner, she could systematically observe and document her own creative process, generating primary data about how sustainable materials impact artistic expression from the artist's lived experience.

<4> Source triangulation for credibility: Casey deliberately combined multiple secondary source types (academic databases, books, online resources) to verify information and avoid relying on a single type of source that might contain specific biases.

Example

Student B: Gentle

Ethical dilemma: Protecting childhood innocence vs real-world exposure and preparation

Research question: 'Should TV shows aimed towards children (from ages 4–7) discuss mature topics (such as violence, current affairs, or discrimination)?'

Organisation

Before starting the project, I broke my research down into subcategories, including:

- stakeholders of the topic (children, parents, educators, show creators, psychologists)<1>
- the practical constraints of presenting children's media (what is seen as suitable for children, how in-depth a topic should be covered)
- who is responsible for what children consume (and should children's media be fully controlled).

I also picked some examples of shows that had interested me. For example, *Sesame Street* uses online videos to cover mature topics that would not have been compatible with a standard televised episode. These guiding topics were useful in some ways and limiting in others. On one hand, by breaking down the issue into specific questions, my research became more specific and thus more manageable. However, this also limited the scope of the issue that I looked at because my subcategories were focused on the creation and distribution of TV shows rather than the impact on children after watching them<2>. Thus, my project ignored other facets of the topic. For instance, many of the sources – from psychological and medical institutions to the Fred Rogers Centre's paper on the matter – state that exposure to TV generally has a negative impact on children's lives. Many of my sources discussed how 'the developmental trajectory of the child matters, and the place and purpose of the media and technology use matters.' (Paciga & Donohue, 2017). However, these matters were not mentioned in my video. To justify this limited scope, I made sure to comprehensively discuss different perspectives on education rather than to generalise perspectives in different areas.

Cultural range

I struggled with finding relevant case studies from different cultures. For one thing, Hong Kong television doesn't make many original children's shows, rather it broadcasts Western shows<3>. Thus, the scope of shows I knew of before this project was limited to shows from North America and England.

To balance out the use of Western shows, I used a survey to collect the opinions of Hong Kong parents. In this way, I hoped to reflect Hong Kong's endorsement of foreign shows while still reflecting local parents' values. I aimed for the survey to be accessible for demographics across Hong Kong, which I tracked by asking what school their children went to. To garner a range of Hong Kong parents, the survey was posted on both a Hong Kong schools' forum and an international school's primary school newsletter. The survey was also available in two languages to make it accessible<4>. However, very few respondents had kids in local schools, meaning that my results were not fully representative of the Hong Kong population<5>.

To ensure a broad range of shows beyond the ones I knew of, I used shows that my interviewees and sources had used as examples. For example, Dr Zhou brought up the German show *Checker Tobi*, which was outside my cultures. Thus, I was able to link my discussion to relevant and diverse examples<6>. However, the range of shows I had was still limited to Western shows – the only exception being localised *Sesame Street* broadcasts (for example, muppets made for specific countries' issues). So although I understand how many western shows have chosen to approach mature topics, my understanding of shows in Africa, Asia and Oceania is extremely limited.

Commentary: Gentle's systematic approach combined multilingual surveys of Hong Kong parents (primary) with secondary sources from psychological institutions, the Fred Rogers Centre, and academic research on child development, allowing her to bridge local cultural perspectives with expert knowledge while navigating the complex stakeholder landscape of children's media.

<1> Stakeholder bias recognition: Gentle explicitly identified different stakeholder groups that would have varying interests and perspectives on the topic, demonstrating awareness that each group might have inherent biases based on their roles and responsibilities.

<2> Scope limitation acknowledgment: Gentle recognised the limitations of her methodological choices and how they might bias her findings toward production perspectives rather than reception effects. This demonstrates sophisticated methodological self-awareness.

<3> Cultural bias compensation: Gentle identified the cultural bias in available show examples and deliberately designed her primary research (parent surveys) to provide local Hong Kong perspectives, demonstrating active efforts to address geographic and cultural limitations in existing sources.

<4> Demographic bias mitigation: Gentle actively worked to prevent selection bias by distributing her survey through multiple channels and providing multilingual access, showing awareness of how access barriers could affect her sample.

<5> Bias limitation honesty: Gentle transparently acknowledges where her bias mitigation efforts fell short, demonstrating research integrity by not overstating the representations of her findings.

<6> Source-driven diversification: Gentle let her expert sources guide her to examples beyond her personal knowledge, reducing the bias that would come from only analysing shows she was familiar with.

Example

Student C: Esha

Ethical dilemma: environmental sustainability vs business and economic viability in culinary industry

Research question: 'Should restaurants be responsible for promoting meat alternatives to prevent climate change?'

'To ensure an unbiased viewpoint, I researched reliable and well-established local news websites like *South China Morning Post*, which are known to publicly publish impartial information. This provided accurate information relevant to local community members. I used trustworthy sources like *Business Insider* and *The New York Times*, reputable for their analysis and credibility on a global scale**<1>**. The quality of their reporting assisted me to attain objective information.

I used articles directly from companies selling meat alternatives, such as Beyond Meat and Impossible Foods, as they provide statistics of their product's environmental impact from within their business. However, there is still bias as they could also manipulate the figures to maintain their corporate image of creating environmentally beneficial consumer products**<2>**. To remain fair and neutral, I used news articles from *Reader's Digest* providing similar facts to the environmental information noted in the aforementioned websites. As they have no affiliation with the companies of these popular meat alternatives, it also allows me to obtain unbiased analytical perspectives on the topic**<3>**.

As for primary research, I chose to interview the manager of a mid-priced restaurant in Hong Kong that sells Impossible Meat**<4>**. It allows me to get first-hand information on how well it performs amongst the primary demographic of people who eat outside, who are typically aged 20–40 years old. It provides me with a unique perspective but nevertheless, it is simply one restaurant and cannot be used as a benchmark for how well meat alternatives could sell across Hong Kong.

Commentary: Esha's strategic source triangulation balanced a targeted interview with a local restaurant manager (primary) with comprehensive secondary research from news sources, company websites, and independent analysis, enabling her to ground global trends in local implementation while maintaining credibility through diverse, well-evaluated sources.

<1> Credibility-based source selection: Esha explicitly chose sources based on their reputation for objectivity and credibility, demonstrating awareness that source selection itself is a bias mitigation strategy.

<2> Commercial bias recognition: Esha demonstrates sophisticated understanding of funding bias and conflicts of interests, explicitly acknowledges that company sources have inherent commercial motivations that could affect their reporting.

<3> Independent source verification: Esha deliberately sought out independent sources without commercial ties to verify information from company sources, demonstrating methodological triangulation to counter potential commercial bias.

<4> Sample size limitation acknowledgement: Esha explicitly recognises the limitations of her single-case primary research and does not overstate its generalisability, showing methodological honesty about potential limitations and bias.

These examples show how successful research methodology depends on matching your approach to your specific research question and available resources. All three learners strategically combine both primary and secondary sources to strengthen their projects. They use secondary sources to establish credibility and provide theoretical foundations, while employing primary research to fill specific gaps, explore local contexts and add unique insights that were not available in existing literature. In addition, each student was honest about their methods' limitations and adapted their approach to their strengths: Casey leverages her artistic skills and access to art communities; Gentle uses her multilingual abilities and local connections effectively; and Esha focuses on building credibility through diverse, well-evaluated sources.

Learning journal entry

Activity

Do a quick self-check of your research approach. Write down the key parts of your preliminary research plan based on the components in the table above.

Finding and evaluating sources

Finding good, reliable information is vital for your reflective project. Knowing how to evaluate sources not only secures the credibility and relevance of your research but also prepares you for your future professional life. In any career – whether in business, the arts, health, engineering or another field – making informed decisions depends on using trustworthy sources. Using unreliable information can damage your reputation, lead to costly mistakes or compromise people's safety and trust.

For example:

- business leaders rely on credible market research to launch new products, understand consumer needs and stay competitive
- engineers and architects evaluate the quality of building materials to ensure safety and compliance, and to confirm that products meet strict regulatory standards before making construction decisions
- health professionals review up-to-date research in medical journals to make life-saving decisions and safeguard patient wellbeing.

The CRAAP test and OPVL method

The CRAAP test helps you judge whether a source is trustworthy by checking its Currency, Relevance, Authority, Accuracy, and Purpose.

Think of the test as a traffic-light system for your sources – it helps you decide if you should go ahead, slow down or stop using a source.

The CRAAP test

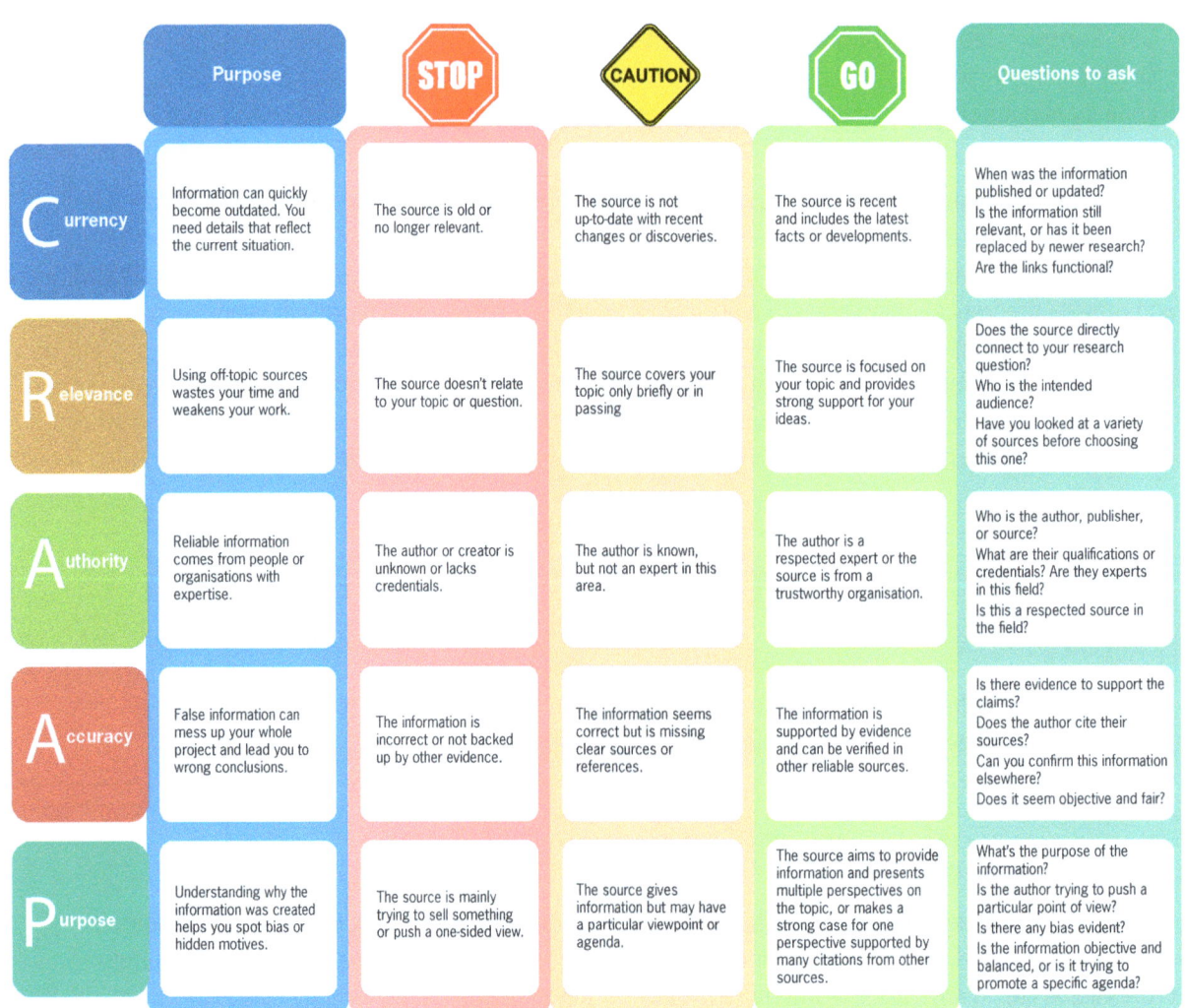

	Purpose	STOP	CAUTION	GO	Questions to ask
Currency	Information can quickly become outdated. You need details that reflect the current situation.	The source is old or no longer relevant.	The source is not up-to-date with recent changes or discoveries.	The source is recent and includes the latest facts or developments.	When was the information published or updated? Is the information still relevant, or has it been replaced by newer research? Are the links functional?
Relevance	Using off-topic sources wastes your time and weakens your work.	The source doesn't relate to your topic or question.	The source covers your topic only briefly or in passing	The source is focused on your topic and provides strong support for your ideas.	Does the source directly connect to your research question? Who is the intended audience? Have you looked at a variety of sources before choosing this one?
Authority	Reliable information comes from people or organisations with expertise.	The author or creator is unknown or lacks credentials.	The author is known, but not an expert in this area.	The author is a respected expert or the source is from a trustworthy organisation.	Who is the author, publisher, or source? What are their qualifications or credentials? Are they experts in this field? Is this a respected source in the field?
Accuracy	False information can mess up your whole project and lead you to wrong conclusions.	The information is incorrect or not backed up by other evidence.	The information seems correct but is missing clear sources or references.	The information is supported by evidence and can be verified in other reliable sources.	Is there evidence to support the claims? Does the author cite their sources? Can you confirm this information elsewhere? Does it seem objective and fair?
Purpose	Understanding why the information was created helps you spot bias or hidden motives.	The source is mainly trying to sell something or push a one-sided view.	The source gives information but may have a particular viewpoint or agenda.	The source aims to provide information and presents multiple perspectives on the topic, or makes a strong case for one perspective supported by many citations from other sources.	What's the purpose of the information? Is the author trying to push a particular point of view? Is there any bias evident? Is the information objective and balanced, or is it trying to promote a specific agenda?

Another useful method is OPVL: Origin, Purpose, Value and Limitations. Using these criteria helps you dig deeper into where your information comes from and how useful it really is.

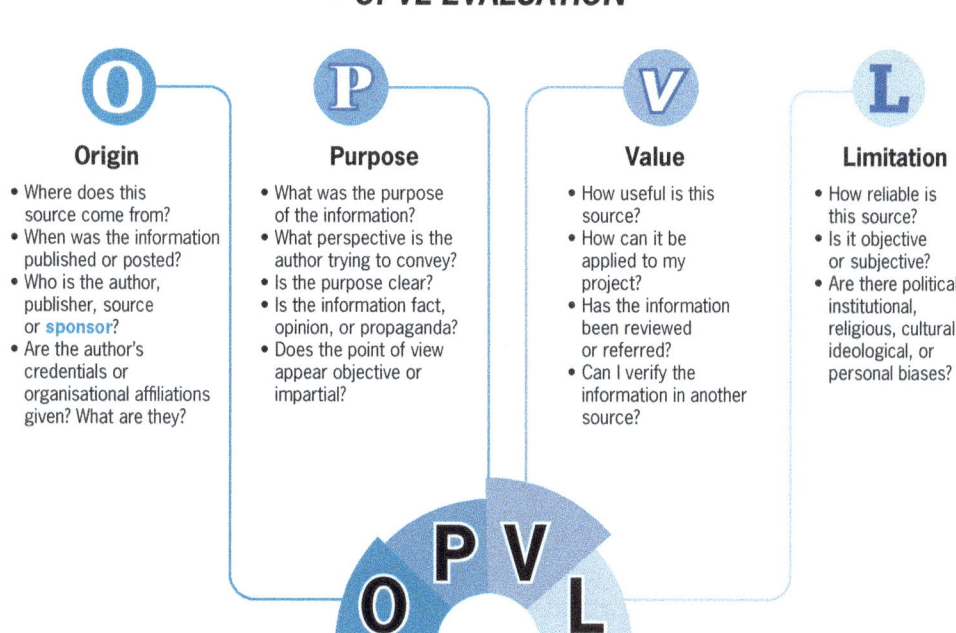

You can develop the OPVL method by summarising your evaluation in the following ways.

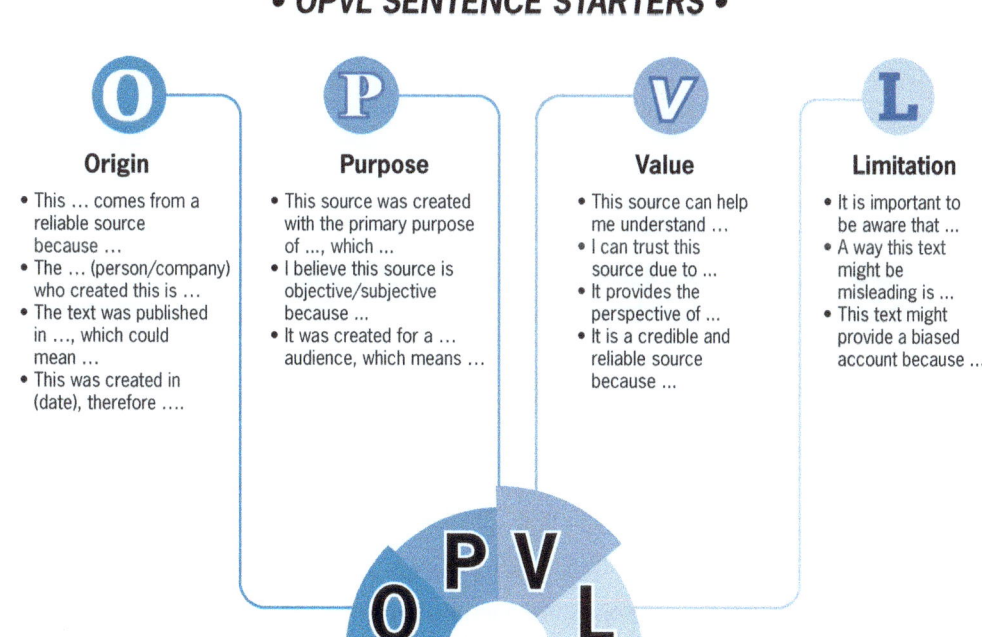

> ## Learning journal entry
> ### Activity
> Gather the sources you have found so far for your research plan. Evaluate them using the CRAAP test or the OPVL process.

Tools for finding reliable sources

Familiarise yourself with the resources available at your school's library or media centre. These may provide access to books, academic journals and digital databases. Ask librarians or media centre staff about the available resources, and how to access them. They can guide you to reliable sources, help you navigate databases and support your research process.

The following are suggestions and examples for where to find trustworthy information for your research.

Academic databases

One of the most effective ways to access credible secondary data.

- Scopus: Covers a wide range of disciplines and provides comprehensive citation analysis.
- JSTOR: Focuses on humanities and social sciences, offering access to academic journals and books.
- PubMed: A key resource for medical and life sciences research.
- IEEE Xplore: Ideal for engineering and technology-related research.
- CQ Researcher: Provides in-depth reports on current issues, offering a balanced view of various perspectives.

Open-access repositories

Free access to research outputs.

- CORE: A collection of **open-access** papers from various repositories and journals.
- PubMed Central: Offers free access to biomedical and life sciences articles.
- Directory of Open Access Journals (DOAJ): A comprehensive directory of open-access journals across various disciplines.

Search engines and aggregators

Specialised search engines and **aggregators** to locate secondary data across multiple sources:

- Google Scholar: A widely used search engine for academic publications.
- Semantic Scholar: Uses AI to help researchers find relevant papers in computer science and biomedical fields.
- CiteSeerX: Focuses on literature in computer and information science, providing free access to scholarly articles.

Government and institutional websites

Many government agencies and research institutions publish valuable secondary data.

- Data.gov: A **repository** of **datasets** generated by the US government.
- World Bank Data: Offers a wide range of economic, social and environmental data.
- Eurostat: Provides statistical information to the institutions of the European Union.

Market research reports

Industry reports from market research firms can provide valuable insights and data.

- Statista: Offers statistics and studies from over 22,500 sources.
- IBISWorld: Provides industry research reports that include data on market conditions and trends.
- Mintel: A leading market intelligence agency that provides insights on consumer markets.

Libraries and information centres

Utilising local or university libraries can provide access to databases and resources not freely available online.

Many local or university libraries offer access to subscription-based databases and archives.

AI-powered tools

Tools to find peer-reviewed sources:

- Otio
- Scite Assistant
- SciSpace
- Research Rabbit

> **Remember**
>
> Using these tools and methods will help you gather solid, credible information that strengthens your research. Remember to always evaluate your sources carefully before including them in your project!

Citing sources

So, you have found some great sources – now you need to give them the credit they deserve.

Citing your sources for an idea, fact, quotation, dataset or image that originates outside your own thinking accomplishes three things:

- It shows your readers where your information comes from.
- It lets them find the original materials easily.
- It demonstrates your academic integrity to avoid **plagiarism**.

By citing sources accurately, you will strengthen the credibility of your project and show respect for the intellectual property of others. There is more information on how to cite sources properly and different methods for referencing in Chapter 7.

Creating an annotated bibliography

An annotated bibliography is a useful tool that summarises each source you use in your research, along with a brief evaluation of why it is important and relevant. An annotated bibliography is essential for managing your independent research and keeping everything organised. It can help you:

- keep track of your research, recording key authors, articles, theories and findings related to your topic
- think critically, analysing how each source fits into your research
- identify potential issues with sources early on

- evaluate the usefulness of each source
- justify your choices, explaining why you included them
- plan your research, highlighting the most relevant sources for your work
- improve your critical thinking in selecting and evaluating sources
- show your engagement with the topic
- make writing easier and more streamlined by focusing on the most relevant and reliable sources.

To create an annotated bibliography, you will need to understand your sources well and think critically about them. Each entry usually includes two parts. The first part is the citation – that is, the full reference for the source, formatted according to a specific style such as APA or MLA. The second part is the annotation – a concise summary and evaluation of the source, including:

- the main purpose, arguments and conclusions
- the intended audience
- the research methods used (if applicable)
- how relevant the source is to your topic
- the strengths and weaknesses of the source
- how it compares to other sources on the same topic.

Try to include a variety of sources in your annotated bibliography, such as books, journal articles, reports and websites.

Writing annotations

✓ Keep annotations concise and clear (3–5 sentences or 150–200 words each).
✓ Focus on the most important aspects of each source.
✓ Use your own words as much as possible.
✓ Provide a critical analysis of the source's strengths, weaknesses and contributions.
✓ Avoid simply repeating the title or copying text from the source.

Remember

By making an annotated bibliography, you will summarise and evaluate your research sources effectively. This helps you remember key ideas and improves your research skills, making it easier to build a strong, evidence-based argument for your ethical dilemma.

Example

Annotated bibliographies

Below are two examples of annotated bibliographies in APA format.

Example 1

Johnson, A. (2019). Exploring Renewable Energy Solutions. *Journal of Sustainable Energy*, 12(4), 123–135.

In this article, Johnson explores various renewable energy solutions, including solar, wind and hydroelectric power. The author, with extensive experience in environmental science, provides a comprehensive analysis of the benefits and challenges associated with each energy source. This peer-reviewed article is credible and offers valuable insights into the potential for renewable energy to mitigate climate change. It will be instrumental in my research, as it supports my argument for increased investment in sustainable energy technologies.

- The relevance and contribution of the source to your research focus.
- Highlights the main purpose and conclusions of the work.
- The source's relation and usefulness to your research.
- The author is a recognised expert in the field.
- Highlights the most important aspect of the source.
- The source is peer reviewed which suggests the author's scholarly work.

Example 2

Garcia, M. (2019). Digital Media and Youth: Understanding the Impact of Social Networks. *Journal of Youth Studies*, 22(4), 567–580.

Garcia explores the effects of social media on youth behaviour and mental health, presenting both positive and negative outcomes. The author, a sociologist with a focus on media studies, uses qualitative data from interviews with teenagers to support her claims. The article is well researched and published in a reputable journal, making it a credible source. This article is relevant to my research on the influence of digital media on adolescent development, providing insights into the complexities of youth interactions online.

- Highlights the focus and scope of the research, and the main findings of the study.
- Points out the author's credentials and the research methodology used.
- Indicates the source credibility.
- Explains how the source is useful for the research and its insights into youth interactions online.

You can also create a table listing your source, descriptions, evaluations and how each relates to your ethical dilemma. The following is an excerpt from a student's annotated bibliography about graphic designers drawing inspiration from existing designs while respecting intellectual property and artistic integrity.

Source	Gordon, C. (2021, May 11). Did this fashion brand rip off Timothy Goodman? PRINT Magazine. https://www.printmag.com/graphic-design/did-this-fashion-brand-rip-off-timothy-goodman/	Macmillan, P. (2024, January 4). The dark original stories behind Disney films. Pan Macmillan. https://www.panmacmillan.com/blogs/general/original-disney-stories-films	Smiley. (n.d.-b). Smiley® Brand Protection: Authenticity & Integrity.
Origin of the source	Design magazine article, PRINT Magazine. This platform is reliable as it focuses on design and visual culture, making it a credible source for topics in the creative industry. It reported the current affairs of the case.	Published blog post, Pan Macmillan, written by Rachel Allen. It is a publishing company showcasing various books across various genres. Pan Macmillan is a trusted publisher for sharing accurate information about books and authors.	The official Smiley Brand website explains its approach to protecting its intellectual property. A reliable source that provides the correct information on Smiley Brand Protection.
Purpose and value	Provides insight into potential copyright infringement issues in the fashion and design industry. It is a neutral article that has been updated. The article examines whether Longchamp may have copied Timothy Goodman's work, presenting facts and figures to support the investigation.	Analyses Disney's reinterpretation of famous fables, adding cultural and historical context to its adaptations – displays a lot of evidence.	This information is reliable, detailing Smiley's legal and strategic measures to protect its intellectual property and brand integrity.
Limitations	The article focuses on one case, and lacks broader industry context. As a magazine article, it does not have the same journalistic objectivity and balance as independent news reports.	Biased: The article's tone is subjective, leaning toward a critique of Disney's creative process, which may influence how readers perceive the company.	The content is likely to be biased toward promoting Smiley's brand and its protection measures. This affects the objectivity of the information presented, as it may prioritise the brand's interests over an impartial analysis of brand protection issues.

Notes/important information	The article discusses intellectual property, fair use, and examines the legal and creative complexities in fashion industry.	A detailed analysis of how Disney's adaptations diverge from the original stories and their broader implications, with credible historical analysis.	The website outlines Smiley's actions and legal frameworks against trademark infringement, and efforts to maintain authenticity and brand identity.
		It offers rich cultural and historical context that enhances understanding of the company's creative choices, highlighting Disney's decision-making and its impact on storytelling.	
		It appears well-researched with historical analysis, making it a more reliable resource for exploring Disney's interpretive process.	
Argument (for/against)	Neutral: Presents both sides of the argument, enabling me to make my own conclusions with more research.	For: Supports the cultural critiques of Disney's copyright practices.	Against: Information is useful, but manipulative and very authoritative – I believe to be unfair.

Learning journal entry

Activity

Create an annotated bibliography for your current sources based on your evaluations.

Understanding ethical research in the reflective project and using AI

Having established your research foundation, you now need to consider the ethical dimensions of your research practice. This includes both academic integrity and the responsible use of technologies such as AI.

Being an ethical researcher is not just about following rules; it is about developing integrity that will serve you throughout your future studies, work and life. In professions like medicine and engineering, misleading research can have serious consequences, so establishing ethical research habits now will serve you well in the future.

There are three key aspects of ethical research:

- Maintaining academic integrity
- Using **AI tools** responsibly
- Conducting research that protects people and the environment.

Academic integrity can be summed up in four key principles:

- **Authenticity:** Your words, ideas and analysis must be your own.
- **Proper citation:** Every time you use someone else's ideas, words or data, you must give proper credit.
- **Accurate reporting:** Report data and findings honestly – never adjust facts to fit an argument.
- **No collusion:** The reflective project is an individual project; inappropriate collaboration is a breach of integrity.

All these principles are explained in more detail in Chapter 7.

Using your learning journal for ethical practice

Your learning journal is a useful tool for maintaining academic integrity throughout your research process. Try to use some of these organisational strategies:

- **Colour-coding:** Use different colours for your own thoughts as opposed to those you have drawn from external sources.
- **Source tracking:** Record full bibliographic details immediately when you find useful sources.
- **Content labelling:** Mark entries as original thoughts, direct quotes, paraphrasing, or summaries.
- **Digital shortcuts:** If you use digital tools, copy and paste bibliographic information that you can easily transfer to your final bibliography later.

> **Remember**
>
> You should cite as you write rather than adding citations later. This prevents accidental plagiarism and makes your final bibliography much easier to compile.

Responsible AI usage: enhancing rather than replacing your work

Having grounded your research in academic integrity and transparent, thoughtful practices, it is time to consider how new technologies, particularly AI, can both enhance and complete your research process.

Technology is a big part of our daily lives, and it is hard to imagine going without it. With the internet at your fingertips, it is natural to turn to online resources for your reflective project. New tools like AI can make your research easier by helping you find, organise, analyse and present information. However, it is important to use AI responsibly – misusing it can put your entire Career-related Programme at risk. In addition to this, AI is changing the way people work at a rapid pace. Experts believe that by 2030, 60 per cent of current jobs will have changed to integrate AI, and new roles will have emerged because of it (University of San Diego, n.d.). So, understanding how to work ethically with AI now will prepare you for a future in which human-AI collaboration is the norm.

> **Remember**
>
> The key principle is that AI should *enhance* your learning and research process, not replace your thinking or writing.

Below are some guidelines to ensure you use AI ethically and effectively in your reflective project.

Dos

- ✓ **Do use AI to enhance your learning:** AI can help you summarise key points and references. Always read and understand these sources yourself, then write your notes in your own words in your learning journal. Think of it as a discussion with your teacher or supervisor.
- ✓ **Do explore different viewpoints with AI:** Ask AI to show you alternative or opposing perspectives on your topic. This can boost your critical thinking and deepen your understanding. You can do this independently or with help from your supervisor or librarian.
- ✓ **Do use AI to improve grammar and sentence structure:** AI tools can help polish your grammar and sentence flow, but do not rely on them to rewrite your entire work. Keep your original drafts for comparison.
- ✓ **Do generate templates or outlines:** Use AI to suggest structures or templates for your project format, but always acknowledge when you do this.
- ✓ **Do seek AI assistance for research ideas and feedback:** AI can suggest new research directions and help expand your scope. It can also give feedback to improve your work, but don't rely solely on it; your supervisor is the best resource for meaningful, context-specific feedback.
- ✓ **Do be transparent about AI use:** If you use AI-generated text, images or graphs, clearly reference the AI tool, including the prompt and date. Add the tool to your bibliography. If AI helped but is not directly quoted, include a brief statement explaining how you used it.
- ✓ **Do use AI to provide evidence of your work's development:** Document your plans and drafts in your learning journal. Save AI-generated information you use to show how your work evolved.

Don'ts

- ✗ **Don't copy quotes from AI without checking source material:** Always read and understand original sources yourself – do not rely on AI-generated quotes without verification.
- ✗ **Don't let AI create your research question:** Work with your supervisor to develop your research question. If AI helps refine it, cite or acknowledge that help.
- ✗ **Don't generate large parts of your project with AI:** Your reflective project should reflect your own thinking and understanding, not AI's.
- ✗ **Don't use AI to write sample work to copy or rewrite:** This is like copying someone else's work and is not allowed.
- ✗ **Don't have AI rewrite your entire project:** Your personal voice should be clear throughout your work.
- ✗ **Don't translate your project using AI:** Writing in one language then using AI to translate can affect the authenticity of your work.
- ✗ **Don't let AI decide your arguments or conclusions:** AI can produce generic or biased content. Use your own critical thinking to form your ideas.
- ✗ **Don't hide your use of AI:** Transparency is key. Concealing AI use violates academic integrity, even if the use was acceptable.

Remember

The IB sees AI as a tool that will become part of everyday learning, like spell check or calculators. The goal is to use AI ethically, keeping your work authentic and original. If you are ever unsure, talk to your supervisor and check your school's policies.

Research ethics: people, safety and environment

Research ethics involves the moral principles and guidelines that govern how to conduct research responsibly. These principles ensure that our pursuit of knowledge does not harm people, animals, or the environment in the process. As a researcher, you have responsibilities that extend beyond simply gathering information; you must also consider the wellbeing of everyone and everything that might be affected by your research activities.

If your research involves other people, you have a responsibility to protect their rights and wellbeing. Essential requirements include:

- Informed consent: Participants must understand what they agree to.
- Right to withdraw: Participants should be allowed to stop participating at any time without pressure.
- Confidentiality: Protect participants' privacy and respect their wishes to preserve anonymity.
- No harm: Your research must not cause anxiety, stress, pain or discomfort to your participants.
- Special considerations: Research with children requires written consent from their parents/guardians.

Remember

Be sure to exercise sensitivity to local, cultural and personal contexts. What might seem normal to you could be inappropriate or offensive to others.

Safety first!

Your safety and the safety of others involved in your research is paramount.

! Follow all safety guidelines provided by your supervisor.

! Never conduct research with participants who cannot respond freely.

! Stop research immediately if anyone shows signs of stress or discomfort.

! Get proper training for any experimental or fieldwork activities.

You should also consider the environmental impact of your research activities. Sustainable research practices include the following:

- Fieldwork: Avoid disturbing natural habitats or ecosystems.
- Travel: Choose sustainable transportation options when possible.
- Materials: Use paper, digital devices, and other resources responsibly.
- Waste: Minimise waste and dispose of materials properly.
- Energy: Be conscious of energy waste when conducting research using digital tools.

Remember

Small choices in your research process can make a significant difference in reducing environmental impact. Every sustainable decision counts. Also, when in doubt, ask. Your supervisor and teachers are there to help you succeed while maintaining the highest ethical standards. Embrace this learning opportunity to become not just a better researcher, but a more ethical practitioner in your chosen field.

Learning journal entry

Activity

Research and list at least three AI tools that can help your research. For each one, note its features, benefits and any limitations.

Refine your project proposal with your updated methodology plan.

Reflection

After learning about the 'dos and don'ts' of AI use, reflect on your understanding of ethical AI usage.

How might you use AI responsibly in your reflective project? List specific dos you will commit to and don'ts you will avoid.

Feedback

Did you receive feedback from your reflective project supervisor or mentor about your intended research methodology?

Document the feedback you have received and consider how you plan to act on it.

Key takeaways: Chapter 5

- Research is the foundation of your reflective project. Gathering, evaluating and using information carefully helps you understand your ethical dilemma thoroughly and supports your analysis.
- You should choose research methods that fit your topic and resources. Primary research lets you collect original data, while secondary research uses existing information. Combining both often gives the best results.
- Evaluate your sources critically. Use tools such as the CRAAP test or OPVL method to check if your information is current, reliable, relevant and unbiased.
- Create an annotated bibliography. Summarising and evaluating each source helps you organise your research, think critically, and justify your choices.
- Use AI responsibly and ethically. AI can support your learning and research but should never replace your own thinking or writing. Always be transparent about your use of AI.

Key terms

aggregator: something that collects related pieces of information from a variety of sources

AI tool: software that uses artificial intelligence algorithms to solve problems and perform tasks

bias: a tendency to prefer one person, thing or idea to another, and to favour that; bias can affect how you see and judge something

collusion: co-operation between two parties that is against the rules or illegal

dataset: a collection of separate sets of information that is treated as a single unit by a computer

mixed approach: an approach to research that combines primary and secondary research; you collect your own data as well as using existing information to get a fuller, clearer picture of your research question.

open-access: referring to publications that are freely available online, with no financial, legal or technical restriction on their availability or use

plagiarism: the act of using someone else's words or ideas and not crediting them

primary research: the process of collecting original data to answer specific questions relating to a study; primary research may be conducted through surveys, interviews, focus groups, observations, experiments or case studies

repository: a place where things are stored, often things that contain knowledge and information

secondary research: the process of analysing existing data that others have already collected; often carried out to gather background information before starting primary research; methods include literature reviews, government reports, books, academic journals, online databases and news articles

sponsor: an individual, organisation, or group that provides financial, technical, or other type of support for a publication, research project, or event; knowing the sponsor can help determine potential influences or biases in the source

survey: a questionnaire used to gather information by asking a sample of people a series of specific questions

Chapter 6 – The research and analysis phase: Analysis

This chapter covers the following:
- Collating your research
- Analysing your research
- Synthesising your research to determine your personal position

Learner profile traits

inquirers

thinkers

principled

open-minded

balanced

reflective

Collating your research

By this point, you have collected a range of valuable primary and secondary sources, and your project should be taking shape. The way you now gather, organise and integrate these materials will influence the success of your final project and your personal position on the ethical dilemma.

Collating research means methodically bringing together information from diverse sources. This involves carefully searching for relevant literature, choosing the best data, evaluating its quality, and combining everything into a clear and meaningful summary or analysis. The goal is to create a solid foundation of evidence that helps you understand your ethical dilemma better and supports your decision-making.

There are three key characteristics of good **collation**:

- Organisation: Your data should be systematically arranged so you can find and use it effectively.
- Comprehension: You should understand how different pieces of information connect to each other and to your ethical dilemma.
- Depth: You should be able to see beyond surface-level facts to understand the underlying values, contexts and implications.

Grouping information and data into categories

Effective collation means grouping your data into meaningful categories based on shared characteristics or themes. Example categories include:

- Stakeholder groups (for example doctors, patients, families, insurance companies)
- Perspectives (supporting your dilemma, opposing it, neutral viewpoints)
- Context (local examples, local examples in a different or distant community, international examples, historical cases)
- Type of evidence (statistics, expert opinions, case studies, personal stories or in-depth interviews)
- Ethical principles (safety concerns, individual rights, economic impacts, government responsibilities)
- To decide which piece of information belongs in which category, first read through each piece of information and ask: 'What is this mainly about?' Next, look for key words and themes that appear

repeatedly across different sources. Finally, consider the purpose of the information: does it explain the problem, show different viewpoints or provide evidence? Remember – some information might fit into several categories.

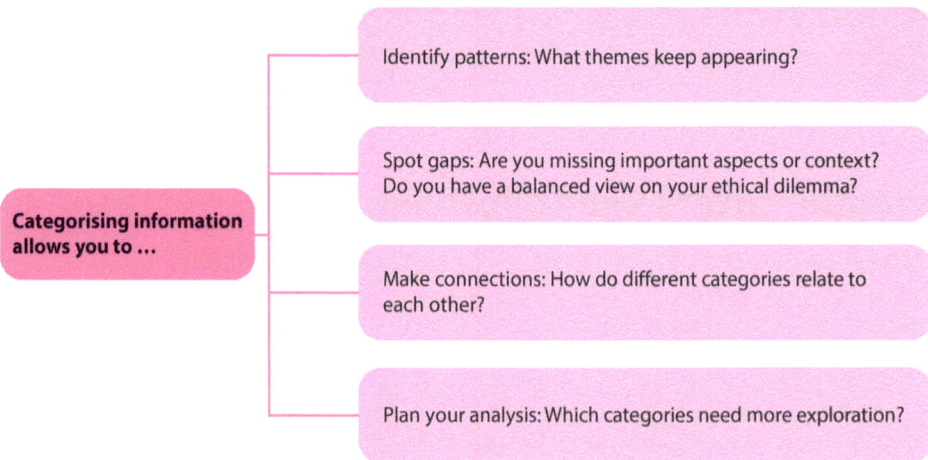

This process allows you to move from simply collecting data to truly comprehending your ethical dilemma, including its wider implications and connections. For example, a dilemma about social media privacy might have wider implications for democracy, mental health, economic inequality, and international relations and policies.

Linking your research to Criterion B

Criterion B of the reflective project assessment criteria measures both the breadth and depth of your research.

Breadth (wide research)	Depth (deep research)
Successful research looks at a broad range of high-quality sources (academic articles, industry reports, news media, official statistics, stakeholder interviews, and so on) that represent multiple perspectives and historical, social, geographic or cultural contexts.	Successful research also requires extensive understanding – evidence that you have gone beneath surface facts to analyse underlying values, causes, and consequences, and that you can explain clearly how specific individuals, groups, or communities are affected by the dilemma.

In practical terms, you need to demonstrate how well you understand the different contexts and issues related to your dilemma. Use the categorisation techniques, as well as the analytical tools explored in the section below, to keep pushing both dimensions to meet – and even exceed – the expectations for Criterion B.

Highest mark-band score	Research	Knowledge and understanding	Impact of dilemma
5–6	The scope and depth of the research are comprehensive. An extensive range of resources is used.	The work indicates extensive knowledge and understanding of issues related to the ethical dilemma.	The work demonstrates excellent understanding of how identified contexts, individuals or groups are impacted by the issues explored.

Note that you can find a breakdown of these expectations, with concrete examples and strategies to guide you on how you can achieve high quality research, in Chapter 7.

Managing and organising your research results

Ethical dilemmas are complex. As you explore different resources, perspectives and contexts, you will start to realise how interconnected everything is. Do not be overwhelmed by this – it is a sign that your research is going well!

Your next step is to make sense of all this information. The sections below outline some models and tools that can help you organise your ideas and connect them to your data. These tools can also expand your thinking and broaden the initial scope of your research. They provide structured ways to organise your thinking, expand your understanding, and see the bigger picture without getting lost in the details. Think of these tools as frameworks that help you build that strong foundation for your analysis systematically, one piece at a time.

Remember

Research is not a straight line from start to finish. As you organise your data you will discover new questions and identify gaps in your understanding. You may need to adjust your focus. This is normal and valuable, so keep an **open mind**, and try to identify a variety of contexts and perspectives to prepare for a comprehensive and in-depth analysis.

Analysing your research

The analytical iceberg model

Because ethical dilemmas are complex, they have obvious parts (what you can easily observe) and hidden parts (underlying values and beliefs). The analytical iceberg model likens ethical dilemmas to icebergs – what you see on the surface is only a small part of the whole issue. Above the waterline you can see visible aspects, such as laws, policies, observable events, public actions, narratives and stated positions. Below the waterline lie hidden aspects such as cultural values, personal beliefs, historical context and underlying assumptions.

(Analytical Ethics, Suzanne Choo, 2023)

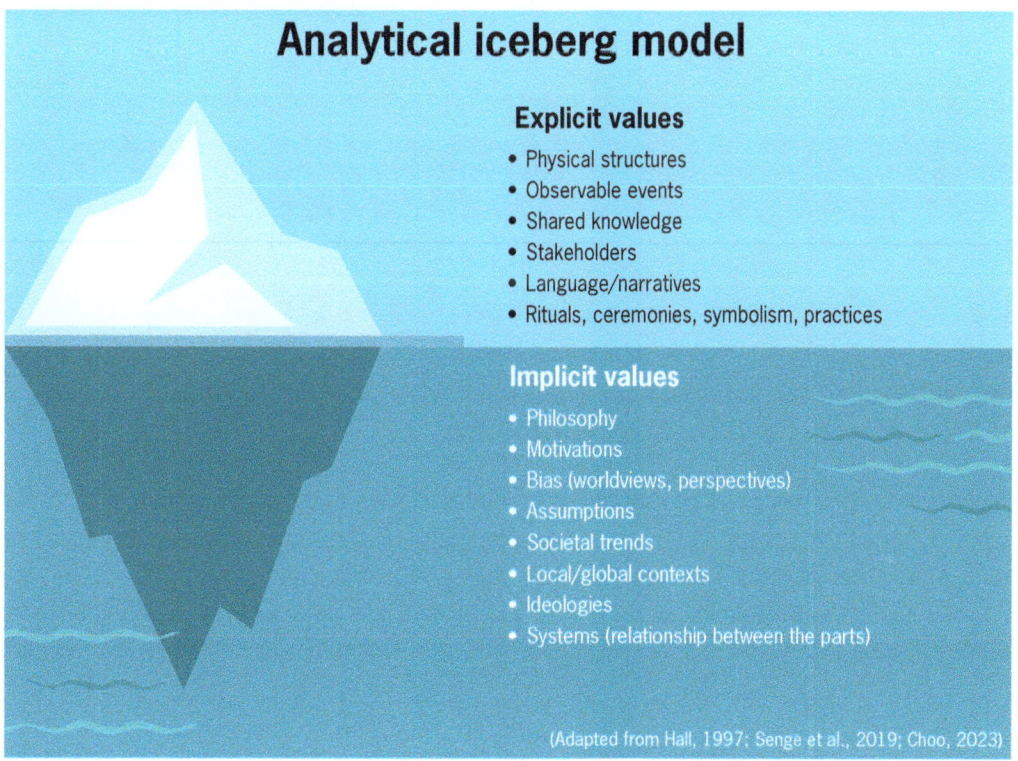

To use the analytical iceberg, follow these steps:

1. Identify the visible aspects of your dilemma – what can everyone see and agree or disagree on?
2. Dive deeper to find hidden aspects – what values, beliefs and assumptions drive different positions?
3. Consider how the hidden aspects influence the visible ones – how do underlying values shape positions?

Example

The analytical iceberg model

Ethical issue: Balancing profit and sustainability in the food and beverage industry

Analytical iceberg model

Explicit values

- Physical structures: Business operations; production facilities and infrastructure; supply chains.
- Shared knowledge: Industry standards; research and development; best practices; stakeholder expectations.
- Language and narratives: Corporate communications; media coverage; marketing and promotional materials; policies and guidelines.
- Observable events: Corporate practices; public commitments; measurable sustainability metrics.
- Stakeholders: Consumers; employees; suppliers; investors; regulators; environmental groups.
- Rituals and practices: Corporate events and initiatives; practices; symbolism; certifications; reporting.

Implicit values

- Philosophy: Corporate profit maximisation; societal obligation; ethical frameworks.
- Motivations: Profit; regulatory compliance; brand reputation; commitment to environmental stewardship.
- Biases or worldviews/perspectives: Feasibility and importance of sustainable practices; corporate and consumer biases.
- Assumptions: Consumer preferences; market demand; regulatory responses; cost and benefit of sustainable practices.
- Societal trends: Social and environmental concerns; corporate responsibilities; changes in regulations and practices.
- Local/global context: Local production practices; global sourcing and distribution; global sustainability norms; resource availability; stakeholder priorities.
- Ideologies and systems (relationships between different parts): The role of business; corporate social responsibility; consumer support; feedback loops.

(Adapted from Hall, 1997; Senge et al., 2019; Choo, 2023)

Cultural differences can impact on consumer behaviour, corporate decision-making, regulatory approaches, and societal expectations

The analytical iceberg model gives a **holistic** and systematic view of this ethical dilemma. You can see and evaluate it beyond surface-level factors such as the physical structure of the industry (business operations, production facilities and supply chains), shared knowledge (industry standards, best practices, stakeholder expectations), and the various stakeholders' perspectives. Below the surface, you realise that other factors contribute to the dilemma, too – consumer preferences, market demand, resource constraints, varying priorities among stakeholders, local production practices, and corporate and consumer biases.

As you can see, deciding your personal position on the ethical dilemma in the example here is complex, as it depends on various contexts:

- Economic contexts: Different countries' economic development levels affect their ability to prioritise sustainability over immediate profits.
- Cultural contexts: Some cultures place higher value on environmental stewardship while others prioritise economic growth.
- Regulatory contexts: Government policies and international agreements create different frameworks for business decisions.
- Technology contexts: Available technology affects what sustainable options are feasible.

The collective cultural traditions of your immediate community also influence your perspective. For example, if you come from a farming community, you might prioritise the economic survival of agricultural families. If you are from an urban area experiencing pollution, you might emphasise environmental protection. If your community has strong traditions of collective responsibility, you might focus on shared solutions, whereas communities emphasising individual choice might prefer market-based approaches.

Each solution will carry its own ethical implications and consequences, so it is important to take a stance. A well-supported argument must ultimately advocate for a clear prioritisation, even if that prioritisation presents its own inherent challenges.

The seven step method for analysing ethical dilemmas

The seven step method is a systematic approach to organising and guiding research effectively. It offers seven questions to help you better understand an ethical dilemma, and is especially useful for identifying the different stakeholders affected by an issue and the ways in which they are impacted. It will also ensure that you do not miss important aspects of a dilemma and provides a clear framework for your analysis.

(Michael Davis, Seven Step Method for Ethical Decision-Making, Online Ethics Center)

Example

The seven step method for analysing ethical dilemmas

Ethical issue: The impact of AI-generated artwork on artists and creative industries and communities

Ethical dilemma

 1 Facts
- AI-generated art threatens human artists, especially concept artists and illustrators.
- There are copyright and ownership issues with AI-generated artwork, including work from deceased artists.
- Using generative AI tools increases creative productivity.
- AI tools are already being used in lines of work relating to the creative industry, such as video game design and graphic design.
- AI art generators allow the physically impaired and artistically challenged to produce decent images.
- AI creates the perception that art is easy to make, so it becomes less valuable.

 2 Ethical issues
- Authorship and ownership: AI-generated artwork blurs the lines of authorship and raises questions about who should be credited as the creator.
- Creative expression and authenticity: AI-generated artwork challenges the creative expression from humans.
- Copyright infringement: AI-generated artworks often rely on vast datasets and copyrighted images without the consent of the original artists, including deceased artists.
- Labour and compensation: AI-generated artwork can impact the livelihood of human artists.
- **Cultural appropriation:** AI algorithms are trained on vast datasets, which may include artwork from various cultures and traditions.
- Transparency and accountability: AI-generated artwork can be used for commercial purposes without clear disclosure to consumers.
- AI-generated images can be used to create misleading content, contributing to the spread of misinformation.

 3 Alternatives
- Fair compensation and support for human artists
- Using stock images and openly licensed or public domain art
- Using ethical AI art platforms such as Adobe Firefly and **Getty images**
- Establishing guidelines and standards – for example, allowing AI use for solely inspirational purposes as a drawing aid
- Transparent attribution and disclosure

 4 Stakeholders
- Artists (art being stolen, threat to career)
- Audiences and consumers of art
- Media/art-sharing sites (where most algorithms are frequently taken from, where art is mostly posted by artists)
- AI developers and companies
- Businesses and commercial entities
- AI generative tools users (both for personal and commercial purposes)
- Regulators and policymakers (government agencies, regulatory bodies, legal entities and copyright organisations)

 5 Ethics of the alternatives
- Equity, inclusion and respect for creative labour
- Balancing inspiration and appropriation
- Balancing innovation and protection
- Economic sustainability and financial viability and instability
- Respect for copyright versus quality variation and lack of uniqueness
- Transparency and accountability versus limited creativity
- Promoting ethical innovation versus implementation challenges
- Informed consumer choices versus complexity of attribution and inconsistency of practices
- Legal clarity and fair competition versus bureaucratic delays and stifling innovation

 6 Practical constraints
- Technology limitations, such as algorithmic bias
- Determining the ownership and copyright of AI generated artwork
- Regulation and enforcement compliance from various users
- Lack of universal ethical guidelines on the use of AI
- Consumer awareness and informed decision-making
- Market competition and economical limitation

 7 Actions
- The best alternative would be commissioning and hiring artists to create art for commercial purposes. For personal reference and as an aiding tool, AI should be allowed. This can be done by creating restrictions on the tool (legal restrictions and disclaimers by the company) and making people sign up to use it (disclaimer for information collection).
- People who use the generator should be aware of the consequences of using it for purposes other than inspiration and personal use.

This structured method allows you to thoroughly evaluate the ethical issue through a series of interconnected steps. You can see how it helped guide this student to lay out the basic facts, clarify AI's influence (including the potential threats to artists, copyright issues and productivity gains), and identify core ethical issues, such as authorship, authenticity, copyright infringement, labour implications, cultural appropriation and the need for transparency.

The model also prompted this student to explore alternatives such as fair compensation models, ethical AI platforms and regulatory guidelines. It encourages them to consider a wide variety of stakeholders, including artists, consumers, AI developers, businesses and regulators. By examining the ethical implications of each alternative, the model reveals inherent trade-offs.

Finally, it emphasises practical constraints, such as technological limitations and enforcement challenges, requiring you to define concrete actions to implement the best alternative with clear justification. Navigating this dilemma necessitates acknowledging the complex interplay of values and advocating for a clear path forward, recognising that any chosen solution will inevitably present its own set of challenges and ethical considerations.

The McGaan box

This approach (also known as the four-box method) breaks down ethical issues into four distinct parts: the situation, the conflicts and values, the traditions and principles, and the decisions. It was originally designed for medical ethics, but its structured approach can be applied to ethical dilemmas across different fields. It is a great way to organise complex dilemmas and consider multiple perspectives.

(University of Washington Department of Bioethics & Humanities)

The McGaan box

The situation	The conflicts and values
The traditions and principles	The decisions

Example

The McGaan box

Ethical issue: Whether artists should compromise their authentic artistic expression to gain visibility on social media platforms

The situation
- Enhanced visibility and exposure
- Networking and opportunity for collaboration
- Direct engagement with audiences
- Marketing and promotion
- Influence of algorithms and trends
- Accessibility and inclusion
- Over-saturation and competition
- Copyright and art theft
- Validation, self-worth and mental wellbeing

The conflicts and values
Conflicts:
- Artistic integrity, the artists' mental health and wellbeing versus popularity
- Authenticity versus curation
- Individuality versus conformity
- Privacy versus exposure
- Artistic growth versus commercial success
- Censorship versus artists' freedom

Values:
- Community and support network
- Accessibility and democratisation
- Integrity and authenticity
- Innovation and self-expression
- Empowerment and self-advocacy

The traditions and principles
Traditions:
- Artistic expression and freedom
- Artistic integrity
- Community and collaboration
- Access and democratisation
- Cultural diversity

Principals:
- Transparency
- Respect for intellectual property
- Authenticity
- Cultural sensitivity
- Artists' mental health and wellbeing

The decisions
- A balanced approach that prioritises authenticity, transparency, self-promotion and self-care.
- Encourage artists to share behind-the-scenes glimpses of their creative process and artistic journey to demonstrate authenticity and transparency. This will foster trust, connection and engagement from the audience.
- Establish clear guidelines for ethical use of social media including the importance of respecting copyright, acknowledging original creator (including AI generated art), and avoiding misleading representations.
- Highlight the balance of self-promotion that builds credibility, reliability and trust.
- Emphasise mental health and wellbeing by setting boundaries.

This structured approach uses the McGaan box to organise the analysis into distinct yet interconnected categories. The 'Situation' box prompts a thorough description of social media's context, including visibility and opportunities, alongside the challenges of saturation and algorithmic influence. The 'Conflicts and values' box acknowledges tensions in social media, such as conflicts between artistic integrity and popularity, or privacy and exposure, while identifying values like supporting creativity through accessibility and democratisation.

The 'Traditions and principles' box encourages consideration of established artistic traditions, such as freedom of expression, alongside ethical principles like transparency and respect for intellectual property. Finally, the 'Decision' box integrates these considerations, advocating for a balanced approach that prioritises transparency, self-promotion and self-care.

> By methodically organising ethical considerations, this method highlights the complexities of social media's impact on artists and will help you towards a well-reasoned, justifiable decision. It emphasises the need for artists to make informed choices and encourages establishing boundaries to protect their mental health and overall wellbeing.

The spider web analytical tool

The spider web analytical tool allows you to explore how the same ethical dilemma can be understood completely differently depending on contextual factors. The thinking behind this model is that ethical dilemmas do not exist in isolation – they are shaped by multiple interconnected factors, including culture, location, time period, economic conditions and personal experiences.

This tool is particularly valuable for examining ethical dilemmas beyond surface level. Think of it like mapping out all the connections in a complex situation, just as a real spider web has threads connecting to many different points. It will help you understand how people's backgrounds, cultures, beliefs and life experiences all connect to shape their views on the same ethical issue. Importantly, this tool will help you see that these factors do not work alone – they create a web of influences that shape people's perspectives.

The tool is made up of three main components:

- The centre of the web represents the ethical dilemma.
- Each thread represents a different contextual factor.
- The web connections show how these factors influence each other and the dilemma.

To use this tool:

1. Place your ethical dilemma at the centre of the web.
2. Identify a few contextual factors that might influence how people view your dilemma and put these in the first 'circle' of the web.
3. For each factor, ask yourself: 'How might this context change someone's perspective on my dilemma?' Weave a further layer to the web by adding the different ways the same dilemma might be viewed differently in different contexts.
4. Look for connections between different factors – how do they reinforce or conflict with each other? – and draw lines to connect them.
5. Identify which elements are **explicit** and which are **implicit** and group them together on either side of the web.

This systematic approach turns complicated ethical questions into something you can analyse step by step. Instead of just listing different groups of people affected by an issue, you can identify the ways in which factors interact with each other, which will allow you to gain a much fuller picture of how real people experience ethical dilemmas in specific situations.

Example

The spider web analytical tool

Ethical issue: Whether the pursuit of winning in sports takes priority over the athletes' wellbeing

Explicit elements:
- Pressure to win
- Commercialisation of sports
- Conflict of interests between team management, agents, healthcare professionals and athlete's health, safety and mental wellbeing

Implicit elements:
- Pressure to perform and meet high expectations
- Financial incentives and rewards tied to winning
- Institutional and cultural norms prioritising winning
- Potential exploitation by coaches, organisations and fans
- Long term physical and psychological consequences of prioritising winning
- Athletes' autonomy and the ability to make informed choices
- Societal values placed on sports and athletic accomplishments
- Tensions between individual athlete's welfare and team/organisational interests
- Inconsistent ethical standards across different sports and level of competition
- Lack of support for athletes' wellbeing

This model illustrates the complexity of the ethical dilemma by highlighting all the different contextual factors that shape the perspectives of the stakeholders in this issue. You can see how identities such as race, class, gender, religion, nationality/ethnicity, age, culture, political affiliation, education and neighbourhood all affect ethical analysis on this subject. The model prompts a deep dive into explicit elements, such as pressure to win, commercialisation, conflicts of interest, racial discrimination and gender stereotypes. It also encourages an examination of implicit elements, including pressure to perform, financial incentives, institutional prioritisation of winning, societal values placed on sports success, exploitation and lack of support for athletes' wellbeing.

By mapping these explicit and implicit elements, the framework demonstrates the significant role identity and culture play in navigating this ethical challenge. Ultimately, coming to a well-reasoned personal position requires advocating for an approach that prioritises athlete welfare, even if that means challenging deeply entrenched cultural norms and institutional practices focused solely on achieving victory.

> ## Learning journal entry
>
> ### Activity
>
> Choose one of the tools or methods above and use it to organise the data you have collected about your ethical dilemma. Did this help you see anything new or think differently about your topic? List your insights.
>
> ### Reflection
>
> Reflect on process: Did you face any challenges while organising your research? How did you overcome them?
>
> Reflect on progress: How did organising and combining your data help you understand your ethical dilemma better?
>
> ### Feedback
>
> Share your progress with your supervisor to seek feedback. How can their feedback improve your research plan and deepen your understanding of the dilemma?

Synthesising your research to determine your personal position

You are now ready for one of the most intellectually rewarding parts of your journey – bringing everything together to form your own reasoned position. This process is closely linked to Criterion C, which evaluates how effectively you can think critically about your ethical dilemma. The highest level of achievement in this criterion requires you to demonstrate:

- thorough analysis of your ethical dilemma using multiple perspectives and contexts
- a well-reasoned personal position that is clearly justified using evidence from your research
- a comprehensive understanding of how your dilemma affects different individuals, groups and communities
- critical evaluation of different viewpoints and their implications.

To excel in Criterion C, you need to move beyond simply presenting information, to show deep analytical thinking about the complex relationships between different aspects of your dilemma. This means showing how various factors connect and influence each other, and using this understanding to develop and justify your own well-reasoned stance.

The table below shows IB's summary of this criterion.

Highest mark-band	Analysis and synthesis of research	Personal position: Reasoning and evidence	Personal position: Justification and impact
7–8	Analysis and synthesis of the research are thorough. Relevant findings are effectively discussed.	A personal position is identified and supported by clear, focused reasoning. There is substantial evidence that the impact or implications of the personal position have been thoughtfully considered.	There is a clear and concise justification of a personal position. There is substantial evidence that the impact or implications of the personal position have been thoughtfully considered.

There is more information on how to use the assessment criteria to your advantage with concrete examples in Chapter 7.

Analysis and synthesis

Think of analysis and synthesis like cooking. Analysis is like examining the individual ingredients before you cook. When you analyse, you are exploring a complex topic or issue in smaller, more manageable parts to understand how everything fits together. You should focus on examining the relationships between these parts and how they connect, much like understanding how salt enhances sweetness or how acid balances richness.

Synthesis is like creating a new dish by combining those ingredients thoughtfully. When you synthesise, you are combining different ideas, findings and perspectives to create a comprehensive and complete understanding, or new insights – just as a chef combines separate ingredients to create something entirely new that is greater than the sum of its parts. They will not just put ingredients together at random; they understand how flavours complement each other, how cooking methods transform ingredients, and how timing affects the result.

Just as you cannot create a great dish without understanding your ingredients first, you cannot synthesise effectively without thorough analysis. And just as analysing ingredients alone will not feed anyone, analysis without synthesis will not lead to meaningful insights about your ethical dilemma.

When analysing your research, ask yourself:

- What are the main arguments or positions on my dilemma?
- What evidence supports each position?
- How do different contexts (cultural, economic, political, and so on) influence these positions?
- What competing ethical principles or frameworks are present?
- How do different stakeholders' interests affect their perspectives?

Synthesis goes beyond analysis by combining information from multiple sources to create new understanding. Follow these steps to synthesis effectively:

- Look for patterns and themes across sources:
    - Do multiple sources agree on certain points?
    - Where do sources disagree, and why might this be?
    - Are there common values or principles that appear across different perspectives?
- Identify relationships between different pieces of information, for example:
    - How do economic factors relate to cultural values in your dilemma?
    - How do cultural norms and traditions influence different stakeholders' perspectives on this ethical dilemma?
    - Do historical events help explain current positions?
    - How do local contexts connect to global trends?
- Create new insights by combining information. For example, instead of just saying 'Source A argues X and source B argues Y', synthesis might look like this:
    - 'While source A emphasises economic benefits, source B's focus on social costs reveals the fundamental tension between profit and community welfare that underlies this dilemma.'
    - 'The difference between source C and D about implementation reflects deeper differences in their assumptions about individual versus collective responsibility.'

> ### Example
> **What synthesis looks like**
>
> Remember Gentle, who chose to focus on the ethical dilemma of whether television shows directed towards young children should discuss mature topics? After analysing her sources, she synthesised her research like this.
>
> Most TV shows aim to either educate or entertain the audience (Zhou, 2020) & (Ofcome, nd). Children's shows often do both, illustrating lessons in a visually engaging way (Zhou, 2020 & Mc Sweeny, 2020). Some shows have used a similar approach when discussing mature topics. For example, many animated shows feature disabled characters. I believe this could be because disabilities can be easily represented visually without divulging into contexts that are too emotionally distressing for children. However, simplifying issues like disability can disassociate some children from the morals they're meant to learn, causing them to take the story literally. A study by Mares & Acosta used an episode of 'Clifford the Big Red Dog' to investigate children's comprehension of TV show morals. The episode in question introduced KC, a three-legged dog, to teach children about disabilities. They found that children often 'found it difficult to identify the moral lesson' and 'took the story at face value, regarding it only as a tale about a three-legged dog' (Mares & Acosta, 2008). This brings the question of whether children are capable of understanding mature topics. As explained, the main goal of discussing mature topics in television should be to educate children. However, if younger children aren't able to differentiate fantasy from reality, they may imitate negative behaviours from TV shows (Boyse, 2010) or even retain none of the morals (Mares & Acosta, 2008). This is where the crux of the ethical question takes place, and controversies have emerged when shows in the past depicted diversity (Kiley, 2020) or discussed challenging experiences such as racism (reverseracism, 2018).
>
> This synthesis combines multiple sources to reveal deeper insights about the nature of the dilemma itself.

Making ethical decisions on your personal position

The ethical thinking tools and models you have explored will help you analyse and synthesise your research findings to identify and justify the position you choose to take on the ethical dilemma. The next step is integrating your newly acquired research knowledge with thoughtful reflective practice to arrive at a well-informed personal stance.

Ethical decision-making means evaluating different options by combining external evidence with your internal moral compass to choose the position that best aligns with both credible research findings and the ethical principles that guide your actions. To establish this personal position, it is essential to be open-minded and to critically examine your own values and **principles**, deepening your understanding of how individual and collective values are formed. This reflective practice not only prepares you to present your viewpoint with thoughtfulness and nuance but is closely tied to the reflexive practices that enable you to align your choices with both credible evidence and your considered ethical stance (see Chapter 2).

Taking a personal stance means reflecting on how you make decisions. Remember that there is rarely one correct or ideal answer to a question based on an ethical dilemma, because decisions are influenced by different contexts and cultures.

Reflexivity encourages you to look inward to understand your own values, beliefs, assumptions and biases and recognise how they influence your responses. It encourages fairer and more **balanced** decisions. By examining shared assumptions and values, you can challenge existing viewpoints and encourage new ways of thinking. This encourages you to become an **inquirer** – questioning societal norms and values that might influence ethical decisions. It also promotes a more **thoughtful** and open-minded approach that acknowledges the complexity inherent in ethical dilemmas. This integrated self-awareness helps you learn from the decision-making process in past dilemmas and consider the wider effects of your decisions. Critical **reflection** also encourages you to think about how your research-informed decisions fit into bigger social and cultural systems. Knowing yourself better helps you understand others' viewpoints, too, and creates a more robust basis for justifying your chosen personal position.

Learning journal entry

Reflection

Ethical decision-making: Why is it important to think about everyone affected by your decisions? How does this influence what you choose to do?

Cultural perspectives: How do different cultures influence an individual's approach to ethical decisions? Think of some examples of how different people might handle the same dilemma differently.

Activity

Use one of the analysis tools to analyse your own ethical dilemma. Organise your research and record your findings in your learning journal. Feel free to explore additional tools from other resources that you find useful. These tools will help you think deeply and clearly about your dilemma as you form your personal position.

Feedback

After finishing your analysis, meet with your supervisor to discuss your ideas and progress. Record the feedback you get and outline an action plan on how you would like to address and act on the feedback received.

Example

Here is an example of a well-structured personal position statement by a student whose ethical dilemma is about whether AI generated artwork should be used for commercial purposes.

After conducting extensive research and applying the 7-step ethical decision-making framework, I have arrived at a position regarding the commercial use of AI-generated artwork.

My stance is that AI-generated work should be permitted for commercial use only under specific ethical conditions that protect artists' rights, ensure transparent practices, and contribute positively to the creative ecosystem.

Through the research process, I recognised that my initial strong opposition to AI art was rooted in my personal connection to the animation industry and fear about my future career prospects. My reflexive analysis revealed that I was viewing this issue primarily through the lens of self-interest rather than considering the broader implications for all stakeholders. This self-awareness helped me approach the research with greater objectivity and openness to diverse perspectives.

I also discovered that my assumption that "All AI art lacks emotion and creativity" was overly simplistic. The research showed me examples like Spider-Man: Across the Spider-Verse, where AI was used ethically as a tool to enhance human creativity rather than replace it, challenging my binary thinking about this issue.

My position draws primarily from consequentialist ethics, focusing on the outcomes and impacts of AI art use, while incorporating elements of deontological thinking regarding duties and rights. I believe we must evaluate AI art based on its consequences for all stakeholders while respecting fundamental rights to creative ownership and fair compensation.

I support commercial use of AI-generated artwork when:

- Ethical sourcing is ensured: AI systems must be trained on datasets where artists have given explicit consent or been fairly compensated, similar to the Spider-Verse model.
- Transparency is maintained: Any commercial use of AI art must include clear disclosure about the AI's involvement in the creative process.
- Human creativity remains central: AI should function as a creative tool that enhances human artistic vision rather than replacing human artists entirely.
- Artists are protected: Strong legal framework must exist to prevent unauthorised use of artists' work in AI training and to ensure fair attribution and compensation.

This conditional approach reflects my core values of fairness, innovation, and respect for creative labour. It acknowledges that technological advancement can benefit society while ensuring that such progress doesn't come at the expense of vulnerable creative workers. My research revealed that many artists (89 per cent in my survey) actually support AI art for personal use, suggesting that the technology itself isn't inherently problematic - it's how we implement and regulate it.

As someone pursuing animation, this position means I would be willing to use AI tools in my work if they meet ethical standards, while advocating for stronger protections for artists in my field. I would support companies that source their AI training data ethically and refuse to work with those that exploit artists' work without consent.

This research has shown me that ethical dilemmas rarely have simple answers. My position may continue to evolve as technology advances and new regulatory frameworks emerge. I remain committed to staying informed about developments in this field and regularly reassessing my stance based on new evidence and changing circumstances.

Learning journal entry

Reflection

Personal position and new understanding: How has your research and analysis changed or deepened your understanding of this ethical dilemma? What position do you take on this dilemma and what evidence from your research can you use to justify it?

Key takeaways: Chapter 6

- Collate your research systematically to help you get organised and prepared for analysis.
- Use ethical analysis tools to guide your thinking. Models like the analytical iceberg, the seven step method, the McGaan box, and the spider web tool help you explore dilemmas from different angles and break down complex ideas to prepare you for ethical decision-making on your dilemma.
- Synthesise findings to create new insights. Move beyond examining individual parts by identifying patterns, themes, and relationships across multiple sources. Combining these perspectives helps you generate a comprehensive understanding and provides the evidence needed to justify your personal position.

Key terms

collation: the process of gathering, organising and bringing together information about your topic from different sources

cultural appropriation: the act of taking or using things from a culture that is not your own, without demonstrating understanding or respect for that culture

explicit: describing something that is stated openly, so it is clear and exact

holistic: dealing with the whole of something, not just a part of it, considering all influencing factors

implicit: describing something that is suggested but which is not communicated directly, so it must be understood by considering other information, including its context

Chapter 7 – The development phase

This chapter covers the following:
- Format options for the reflective project
- Using appropriate structural and stylistic conventions
- Outlining and organising your ideas
- Creating an initial draft
- Citations and referencing
- Academic integrity
- Reviewing your draft
- Using the assessment criteria to self-evaluate your project
- Feedback and revision

Learner profile traits
Knowledgeable

Thinkers

Balanced

Communicators

Principled

Reflective

Format options for the reflective project

With your research analysed and synthesised and your personal position clarified, it is time to organise your ideas and **communicate** them to others. Before jumping into project development, you should review the requirements for the format you have chosen and be aware of the structural and stylistic conventions of your format choice. These decisions will impact how you create your first project draft.

In Chapter 4, you were introduced to the different formats in which you can present your reflective project. You can find the full requirements for each of the four format types – written, visual, audio and audio-visual – in the IB guidance, but some of the key points are outlined below.

Written format options

In written format, your reflective project will need to take the form of an essay of no more than 4,000 words, including a maximum of 1,000 words for the written reflection. You can choose whatever type of essay you want, but you will probably find that an **expository essay** is most appropriate – that is, one that informs the reader about a topic, or explains something to them. Your essay does not have to be **dissertation**-style (although it can be); essays can take many forms, including proposals, blog posts, newspaper articles and even formal letters.

> **Remember**
> In your essay, make sure you explore your ethical dilemma thoroughly, and cite all your sources properly.

Visual format options

If you prefer a visual format for your reflective project, this might take the form of a photo essay or a storyboard outlining a film or media campaign, for example. It needs to be made up of between five and 15 images that work together to describe or comment on the ethical dilemma you have chosen. They should be accompanied by descriptions or annotations totalling 500–2,000 words that explain what the images show, why you chose them and how they contributed to your project.

Audio format options

There are several options for creating your reflective project as an audio presentation – for example, you might create a podcast, deliver an informative speech or conduct an interview. Whichever you choose, it should be 10–15 minutes long and accompanied by any necessary explanations or context in written form. If you choose the audio option, it is important to explain in writing the inclusion of any music or sound effects.

Audio-visual format options

The options for an audio format above could also work as an audio-visual presentation. In addition to those, audio-visual options include short films or documentaries, video-recorded presentations, and so on. These too should be 10–15 minutes long and accompanied by written explanations or annotations where necessary, and again you should explain your choice of music, visual or sound effects.

> ### Remember
> For the audio and audio-visual formats, you should provide a transcript of your audio presentation in the appendix to your project, but this will not be marked or included in the word count.

> ### Learning journal entry
> #### Reflection
> What format did you choose during the planning phase? Why?
>
> How does it connect to your dilemma and your career of interest?
>
> Are you still enthusiastic about your format choice? If not, what other format would you consider?

Using appropriate structural and stylistic conventions

The biggest differences between the formats are their structural and stylistic conventions. While most formats include an introduction, body and conclusion, there are also individual features and elements unique to each format. Understanding these conventions will create a framework for the structure and **tone** of your reflective project, allowing you to connect with your intended audience and communicate your ideas effectively, with clarity and purpose.

Structure means how you organise the content of your project. This refers to things like formatting, space breaks and **dialogue tagging**, as well as whether you use features such as chapter headings, titles and subtitles. Structural conventions also include grammar, punctuation, spelling, capitalisation, paragraphing and citation styles.

Style refers to the distinctive way in which you express your ideas through word choice, sentence structure, figurative language and other language elements. Some stylistic conventions include **diction** (word usage), **syntax** (sentence structure), tone and **point of view**. Whichever format you choose, stylistic conventions lend coherence and sophistication to your text.

> ## Remember
>
> In the assessment criteria, structural and stylistic elements are linked to Criterion D. However, regardless of your technical skill, Criterion D is focused on the clarity and organisation with which you communicate your ideas. The other assessment criteria – which make up most of your final grade – focus on depth of research, analysis of the dilemma and justification of the personal position you have taken.

The following table outlines some examples of stylistic and structural elements common to a variety of formats. Each format allows for a unique approach to presenting information, drawing conclusions and prompting reflection.

Format	Purpose	Audience	Language	Structural elements
Blog post	To share opinions, insights, reflections, or information on specific topics	General public – online readers looking for information, advice or personal views	Informal, personal, engaging, conversational and **reflective**	Use of headings and bullets, introduction, personal **anecdotes**, ethical analysis, concluding thoughts
Podcast	To entertain and inform on various topics through engaging discussions	General public interested in audio or audio-visual content on diverse subjects	Conversational, informal, engaging, factual	Episodes, **segments**, interviews, discussions, dialogue, transitional music
Speech	To inspire, inform, or provoke audiences with innovative ideas or stories	Broad or specific audience, in person or online viewers seeking inspiration, personal insights, or **call to action**	Engaging, persuasive, clear, personable, narrative	Introduction, main idea or personal story, key arguments, insights, conclusion, call to action or reflection, thank audience for attending/listening

Format	Purpose	Audience	Language	Structural elements
Business proposal	To persuade stakeholders to support a project or idea, or to take action	Business professionals, investors, decision-makers, clients, or organisation leaders	Formal, professional, persuasive, concise, factual and data-driven	**Executive summary**, problem statement, proposed solution, budget, call to action, and conclusion
Field report	To document and analyse real-world observations and findings from a specific field study	Researchers, academic audiences, policy makers, or stakeholders in the studied area	Factual, objective, analytical, formal and evidence-based	Title, **abstract**, introduction, methodology, observations/findings, analysis, conclusion, and recommendations
Documentary	To inform and educate audiences about real-life events or issues	General public or specific audiences interested in the documentary topic	Factual, visual engaging, narrative, artistic, informative, concise	Visual narrative, **voiceover**, music, video **footage**, concluding remarks
Photo essay	To tell a story or convey a message through a series of images	Broad audience, visually oriented, interested in human stories	Visually driven, minimal text, emotionally resonant, impactful	Introduction, series of photos with captions, thematic arrangement, conclusion

Remember

Always use appropriate terminology, structural elements and conventions of style to clearly express the ethical dilemma through your chosen format option. For example, make sure that your project effectively imitates the look and feel of your chosen format and that your tone and communication style are targeted towards your intended audience and purpose. Often, the audience is the general public, but you can also imagine yourself as a career practitioner and aim your project at a specific group or organisation.

Learning journal entry

Activity

Make a list of the stylistic elements you will need to include as you develop your project.

Reflection

How comfortable are you with the structural and stylistic conventions for your chosen format?

Are there any that you feel unsure about? How could you increase your confidence in applying these features?

When preparing for your reflective project, spend some time exploring real-world examples of the format you have chosen, using a table format to research and analyse them. Ideally you would compare at least three examples. This type of analysis of the similarities and differences between examples will help you decide how to approach your own project. Keep in mind that you may need more time to produce your project if you are not already skilled in that format.

Example

Format analysis

Here is an example of a completed format analysis for a graphic novel. Note that the different graphic novels analysed might have slightly different purposes or audiences, and those differences are also reflected in the type of language used, because authors always attempt to communicate in a way that connects to their specific audience and purpose. However, also note that, while there are some variations in the structure, there are more similarities than differences – this is because each format has some standard structural conventions (in this case, sequential visuals made up of illustrations or drawings to tell a compelling narrative story).

Format	Purpose	Audience	Language	Structure
Graphic novel *Maus: A Survivor's Tale* (Volume I: My Father Bleeds History), by Art Spiegelman 1986	To document, educate and bear witness to traumatic family history during the Holocaust	Adult and young adult readers; those interested in history or memoir	Conversational, uses animals as characters to tell story; understated tone	Sequential panels, black and white art; interwoven timelines; present-day and historical narrative; use of visual metaphor
Graphic novel *Smile* by Raina Telgemeier, 2010	To document and normalise the awkward experiences of adolescence, particularly dealing with physical challenges and social acceptance	Middle grade to young adult readers; those who have experienced dental/medical trauma or social challenges in school	Conversational and age-appropriate; relatable teenage voice, uses humour to address serious topics	Chronological narrative following several years, bright, colourful cartoon-style art; clear panel progression; visual metaphors for emotional states
Graphic novel *American Born Chinese* by Gene Luen Yang, 2006	To explore cultural identity and the challenge of belonging between two cultures	Young adult readers; those from immigrant families or dealing with cultural identity issues	Accessible yet sophisticated; incorporates elements from Chinese folklore; uses different narrative voices	Three interwoven storylines that converge; blend of realistic and mythological elements; varied panel styles to distinguish narratives

> ## Learning journal entry
> ### Activity
> In your learning journal, create a table like the one in the example and analyse at least three examples of the format you have chosen.

> ## Remember
> If you are still unsure whether the format you have chosen is right for you, you can also use this template to review and compare several different types of formats to help you decide what works best. Be sure to also talk with your supervisor if you are thinking of switching formats at this point.

Outlining and organising your ideas

While your chosen format will dictate the structure of your project to some degree, the main purpose of every project is the same: to explore an ethical dilemma through various contexts and perspectives, to share your research and to identify your personal position and its potential impact. As such, regardless of format, your reflective project should be structured in a way that communicates your ideas clearly and effectively. To achieve this, you must ensure that your ideas are well developed, focused and connected, and that they flow logically and coherently, so that your reader or listener can follow your reasoning.

Before you begin writing or developing your project, spend some time reflecting on your research, the connections you have made between contexts or perspectives, and the conclusions you have drawn to arrive at your own personal position. From these reflections you will be able to develop an outline that will guide you through your project's development.

> ## Learning journal entry
> ### Activity
> Review your research notes. What connections do you see?
>
> Refer to your activities in Chapter 6. What does your analysis of the ethical dilemma suggest?
>
> ### Reflection
> How might you organise all these ideas in a clear, concise way?

Creating an outline

While it may seem like extra work up front, an outline will ultimately make the project development smoother and easier. This outline will be for your own reference, so it does not have to follow any specific format. However, you should make sure that it sets things out clearly as a kind of roadmap to support your project's structure and development from beginning to end.

A standard outline includes an introduction, key points (with both main ideas and supporting details) and a conclusion. Within that, though, you can organise your ideas in a variety of ways, which may depend on how you want to lead your reader or listener to understand your research and your thinking, so that they arrive at the same conclusion as you do. Some possible organisational structures are:

- chronological
- in order of importance/significance
- cause and effect
- problem and solution
- spatial (for visual or audio-visual formats).

Whichever you choose, your approach should remain consistent throughout the project.

It is also important to use **transitions** between ideas to connect them. Transitions signal relationships between ideas and can be very helpful in moving from the explanation of one context or perspective to another.

Example

The transition words you choose will depend on the relationships between the ideas you are connecting and the organisational approach you are using. Some examples are shown in the table below, but there are many others.

Transition words/phrases	Indicates…
however / conversely / on the other hand	a contrary or opposing idea
therefore / as a result / consequently	a result or effect
firstly / secondly / lastly	an order of ideas
moreover / in addition to / furthermore	an additional idea or elaboration on an idea
for example / such as	an illustration of an idea
similarly / likewise	similar ideas
in conclusion / in summary	the summation of ideas

Remember

All your ideas should be supported with evidence from your research and flow logically towards your conclusion. The conclusion should emphasise your personal position and include discussion of how your decision might impact you, others and your future studies or your career field. This logical flow will make your ideas more cohesive.

Adding details

Once you have decided on the initial direction and organisation of your ideas, you can expand your outline with additional details about your content and any stylistic conventions you plan to use. The more you refine your outline, the easier it will be to create the first draft of your reflective project.

The following examples show how you can use an outline to organise and structure your ideas, using the same ethical dilemma for five different formats: a dissertation-style essay, a podcast, an interview, a speech and a documentary film. Each example relates to an ethical dilemma about algorithmic bias in facial recognition technology.

Research question: Is it ethical to use facial recognition technology?

Conflicting values related to the dilemma: Convenient technology tool to support public safety and security vs individual right to be free from discrimination and wrongful accusation, bias and injustice.

Personal position: While offering convenience and security, facial recognition technology has been shown to exhibit algorithmic biases based on race, gender and age. This raises significant ethical concerns regarding fairness, equity, privacy and potential for discrimination. For this reason, facial recognition technology should not be used in most contexts, as it often leads to discrimination and profiling of certain groups of people.

Example 1
Dissertation-style essay (written)

1 Introduction

A Hook

Start with a compelling real-world example of algorithmic bias in facial recognition leading to misidentification or unfair outcomes.

B The ethical dilemma as a research question

Clearly articulate the ethical dilemma of algorithmic bias and its potential for harm and injustice. Connect it to your career field.

C Background – knowledge from research

Introduce facial recognition technology and its increasing prevalence in various contexts (for example, public safety, security, marketing, consumer technology).

- Defining algorithmic bias: Explore different definitions and types of bias that can occur in AI systems.
- Sources of bias in facial recognition: Analyse the various stages in which bias might be introduced (data collection, labelling, algorithm design, deployment).
- Societal impacts of biased facial recognition: Review existing research on the disproportionate effects on specific demographic groups, particularly in areas such as public safety and surveillance.
- Legal and ethical frameworks: Examine current laws, regulations and ethical guidelines related to AI and facial recognition, highlighting their limitations in addressing bias.

D Scope of essay

Outline the contexts and stakeholder groups that you will examine. This will serve as a transition to the next section of your essay.

2 Exploring diverse contexts

A Context 1

Analysis of an everyday context that most readers will understand (for example, consumer technology and everyday applications).

- Description of the context (for example, smartphone unlocking, social media tagging, personalised advertising).
- Discuss potential biases in everyday applications and their implications for user experience and equity.
- Analysis of how bias can lead to inconvenience, exclusion or even subtle forms of discrimination.
- Impact on stakeholders: Users in certain geographic areas (limited access in rural or low-income areas) users with common demographic features (frequency of mis-identification leading to frustration), technology companies (benefits of use, risk of user dissatisfaction, ethical concerns).

B Context 2

Public safety and criminal justice.

- Description of the context and its relevance to facial recognition.
- Analysis of how algorithmic bias manifests in this context (for example, improved safety data offset by higher misidentification rates for minority groups).
  - Security and access control: Explore cases where the technology has failed to accurately identify individuals.
  - Impact on stakeholders: Individuals wrongly identified; security agencies (trust, effectiveness); communities (fear, injustice).

3 Perspectives of key stakeholders

A Technology developers and engineers

Their perspective on the challenges of creating unbiased algorithms, the technical limitations and potential solutions.

B Security officers

Their perspective on the advantages of using technology to facilitate their work and potentially prevent crime as well as their concerns for both personal and public safety and their desire for public trust.

C Policymakers and regulators

Their perspective on the need for legal frameworks, ethical guidelines and oversight mechanisms.

D Civil rights organisations and advocacy groups

Their perspective on the potential for discrimination and the need to protect vulnerable populations.

E Affected individuals and communities

Their lived experiences and perspectives on the impact of biased facial recognition on their lives and rights.

4 Analysis and evaluation

A Synthesis of findings across contexts

Identify common threads and differences in how algorithmic bias manifests itself and the impact across the chosen contexts.

B Evaluation of ethical frameworks

Analyse existing ethical principles (for example, fairness, justice, autonomy, beneficence, non-maleficence) in relation to the ethical dilemma.

C Consideration of counter-arguments

Acknowledge and analyse different perspectives or arguments that might downplay the significance of algorithmic bias or emphasise the benefits of facial recognition.

5 Conclusion and personal position

A Restatement of the ethical dilemma

Briefly reiterate the core issue.

B Summary of key findings

Summarise the main points of your analysis across contexts and stakeholder perspectives.

C Articulation of personal position

Clearly state your informed personal position on the ethical dilemma, supported by evidence and reasoning from your research. This should go beyond a simple 'yes' or 'no' and demonstrate nuanced understanding.

D Implications and recommendations

Discuss the broader implications of your findings and offer potential recommendations for addressing the ethical challenges identified. This could include suggestions for policy changes, technological development or public awareness initiatives.

E Reflection on learning

Reflect on how your understanding of the ethical dilemma has evolved throughout the research process and how it connects to your career-related studies and future aspirations.

6 Appendix

Bibliography/works cited (list all sources used in your research).

Remember

A written text can include up to five graphs or images if they are useful for supporting the argument. In the example above, the project might include data charts, images with examples of inaccurate facial recognition, or a visual comparison of faces recognised – one correctly and one incorrectly.

Example 2

Podcast (audio or audio-visual)

1 Episode title

'The face of injustice: Is it ethical to use facial recognition technology?'

2 Research question integration

This podcast could be imagined as one in a series. If so, you may want to introduce the episode with a tagline for the imagined podcast series, or may choose to use an anecdote, quote or statistic to introduce the topic. Either way, be sure to clearly state the research question.

3 Format

This podcast could take an investigational approach and could include guest 'stakeholders' to share their perspective, or it could achieve the different stakeholder opinions through audio clips or references to sources and examples. Adjust the timing based on your research/content but ensure the podcast fits the time limit of 10–15 minutes.

4 Outline

Intro music and host introduction (1 minute)

Briefly introduce the topic and the research question. Connect the topic to the relevant career field.

Segment 1: Set the scene – How is facial recognition used in different contexts? (2 minutes)

- Briefly introduce two or three key contexts (for example, public safety, marketing, everyday consumer technology).
- Give brief examples or scenarios to illustrate the use of facial recognition in these contexts.
- Pose initial questions about fairness within each context.

Segment 2: Stakeholder perspectives – Who does this impact? (3–4 minutes)

- Discuss (or share short audio clips, real or simulated) the perspectives of different stakeholders. For example:
    - a technology developer discussing the challenges of bias
    - a security officer sharing how they use facial recognition
    - a civil rights advocate expressing concerns about discrimination
    - an individual who has experienced misidentification
    - a policymaker discussing potential regulations.
- Analyse how each stakeholder's perspective informs the ethical dilemma.

Segment 3: Unpack the bias – Why does this happen (2–3 minutes)

- Briefly explain the technical reasons behind algorithmic bias in an accessible way.
- Use analogies and clear language to discuss biased data and algorithm design.
- Briefly connect this back to the research question – how does this technical issue impact fairness and equity?

Segment 4: Reflect on the impact (2–3 minutes)

- Discuss the real-world consequences of biased facial recognition in your chosen context.
- Analyse the impact on individuals, communities and institutions.
- Encourage listeners to consider the ethical implications.

Segment 5a: Personal reflection and position (2–3 minutes)

- The host(s) shares their personal reflections on the ethical dilemma based on the research.
- They clearly articulate their personal position on the research question, supported by the evidence discussed.
- Offer potential solutions or ways forward.

Segment 5b: Conclusion and call to action (1 minute)
- Summarise the key points and reiterate the research question.
- Encourage relevant stakeholders to take appropriate action based on your recommended solution(s).
- Outro/closing music and credits.

5 Additional written content

Provide a few paragraphs that outline your ethical dilemma, how it relates to your career field, a brief explanation of the format for your podcast (explain any music, visual or sound effects as appropriate) and any essential explanation of your research or other information that was not adequately reflected in the podcast.

6 Appendix

Bibliography/works cited and a copy of the podcast transcript.

Remember

Make sure you do not exceed the total word/time limit – for example, a 10-minute podcast is roughly 1,500 words, and a 15-minute podcast is roughly 2,250 words. When combined with any additional written information, the total should not exceed 3,000 words so that you still have 1,000 words remaining for your final written reflection. If you exceed 3,000 words, you will have to reduce your written reflection, which could impact your achievement level for Criterion E.

Example 3

Interview (written, audio or audio-visual)

1 Title

'Decoding discrimination: A conversation with an expert on whether the use of facial recognition technology is ethical.'

2 Research question integration

The interviewer should explicitly state the ethical dilemma research question at the beginning and guide the conversation to address its different aspects.

3 Outline

Introduction by the interviewer (2 minutes)

Introduce the topic, the research question and the expert, highlighting their relevant experience and perspective within their field (for example, a legal scholar specialising in technology law, the local chief of police, an airport security officer).

Contextualising the dilemma (3 minutes)
- Interviewer: 'Dr/Chief/Mr/Ms [expert's name], can you explain the ethical challenges posed by algorithmic bias in facial recognition within the specific context of [expert's area]? How does bias in this technology intersect with principles of fairness and equity in public safety?'
- Expert provides insights and examples.

Stakeholder perspectives (3-4 minutes)

- Interviewer: 'From your perspective, how do different stakeholders – such as security officers, policymakers, individuals and technology developers – view and experience the impact of this bias? Are there conflicting perspectives?'
- Expert shares insights on various viewpoints.

Implications of bias (3 minutes)

- Interviewer: 'What are the underlying causes of this algorithmic bias, and what are the most significant societal ramifications, particularly concerning fairness and equity?'
- Expert elaborates on the technical and social aspects.

Towards ethical implementation (3 minutes)

- Interviewer: 'Considering the complexities, what steps or considerations do you believe are crucial for a more ethical implementation of facial recognition technology, addressing the issues raised by our research question?'
- Expert offers potential solutions and recommendations.

Conclusion and personal reflection/position (3 minutes)

- Thank the expert(s) for their insights and reiterate key takeaways.
- Interviewer: 'Based on my research and the discussion with our expert(s), my personal stance on the ethical dilemma is…'.
- Share any call to action or concluding thought.

5 Additional written content (if an audio or audio-visual interview)

Provide a few paragraphs that outline your ethical dilemma, how it relates to your career field, who your expert is and why they were selected, and any essential explanation of your research or other information that was not adequately reflected in the interview. For example, if due to time constraints the interview focuses solely on the expert's opinion, you will need to express your personal position and reasoning in the additional written content. Ensure that the total time/word count combined does not exceed the maximum allowed.

6 Appendix

Bibliography/works cited. If it is an audio or audio-visual interview, you must include a copy of the transcript.

Remember

You can interview actual experts, or you can write an interview script based on quotations and information from your research, having another person respond using your script. The interview could be a one-to-one interview or a panel discussion, but your format must accommodate word and time limits (10–15 minutes for audio/audio-visual or a total of 3,000 words). You could ask one question specifically to each panel member or be very intentional about the interaction of panel members to address the perspectives and contexts from your research.

Example 4

Speech (audio or audio-visual)

1 Speech title

'About face… Questioning the ethics of facial recognition use.'

2 Research question integration

Clearly state the research question early in the speech and reiterate it at key points.

3 Format/tone and audience

A persuasive speech delivered to a community forum.

4 Outline

Opening (1–2 minutes)

- Start with a compelling anecdote or statistic highlighting the use and potential pitfalls of facial recognition in a specific context relevant to your career interest.
- Introduce the research question as the central focus of the speech.
- Briefly state your initial connection to the ethical dilemma.

Contextualising the issue (3–4 minutes)

- Briefly describe two or three related contexts where algorithmic bias in facial recognition has significant ethical implications (for example, border security, access to services, social media).
- Provide concise examples of how bias manifests in each context, including its positives and its potential to undermine fairness.

Stakeholder perspectives (3–4 minutes)

- Briefly present the perspectives of key stakeholders (for example, individuals in favour of its use, as well as those affected by misidentification, technology developers grappling with bias, policymakers considering regulations, security officers using the technology).
- Emphasise how these different viewpoints contribute to the complexity of the ethical dilemma.

Analysis and synthesis of research (3 minutes)

- Explain the fundamental reasons behind algorithmic bias (data limitations, design choices) in a concise way that is accessible to the audience.
- Directly link these reasons back to the research question – how do these technical issues impact fairness and equity?

Personal position and call to reflection (2–3 minutes)

- Clearly articulate your personal position on the ethical dilemma, drawing on the research, contexts and stakeholder perspectives you have discussed.
- Support your stance with reasoned arguments linked to evidence.
- Encourage the audience to critically reflect on the ethical implications of facial recognition technology in their own lives and future careers.

Conclusion (1–2 minutes)

- Reiterate the research question and your personal position.
- End with a powerful, memorable statement that leaves the audience thinking about the ethical implications of this technology.
- Thank the audience for their attention.

5 Additional written content (optional but recommended)

Even though for a speech there are likely no images, music or sound effects used, you can provide a few paragraphs that outline the context for your speech, your ethical dilemma, how it relates to your career field, and any essential explanation of your research or other information that was not adequately reflected in the speech. Ensure the total time/word count combined does not exceed the maximum allowed.

6 Appendix

Bibliography/works cited. Whether this is an audio or audio-visual, you must include a copy of the audio transcript.

Remember

Adjust your tone and focus depending on your audience (for example, public hearing, policymakers, informative Ted Talk style speech). Adjust your timing depending on your research and flow of the speech, allowing for appropriate pauses. Be sure to use eye contact and dynamics with the volume and emphasis of your voice – even if you are speaking to a camera/imaginary audience instead of a live audience.

Example 5

Documentary film

1 Film title

'The algorithmic shadow of facial recognition: Is its use ethical?'

2 Research question integration

The research question should be visually presented early in the film and revisited through narration.

3 Outline

Opening sequence (1–2 minutes)

- Visually engaging montage showcasing the widespread use of facial recognition technology across different contexts and in everyday life (smartphones, security cameras, airport security footage, job interview clips, social media interfaces).
- Juxtapose this with subtle visual cues hinting at potential flaws or inequalities (for example, glitches on certain faces, news headlines about misidentification).
- Introduce the central research question through on-screen text and briefly hint at the underlying ethical complexities. Use text or narration to ask 'Is this technology truly objective? Is it always accurate?'

Act 1: Contexts of application (2–3 minutes)

- Explore two or three distinct contexts where facial recognition is used (for example, healthcare access, urban surveillance, online identity verification).
- Use visual examples and brief interviews or voiceover narration to illustrate the technology in each context.
- Raise initial questions about potential biases and their impact on fairness within these settings.

Act 2: Impact (2 minutes)

- Feature interview clips/information about relevant current events or individuals who have experienced the negative consequences of algorithmic bias in facial recognition (for example, difficulty accessing services, wrongful suspicion).
- Visually represent their experiences and emotional impact.
- Highlight the human cost of the ethical dilemma.

Act 3: Decoding the bias (2 minutes)

- Show interview clips with technology developers and AI researchers (or use narration) explaining the technical reasons behind algorithmic bias.
- Use visual aids (graphics, animations) to illustrate concepts like biased datasets and algorithmic design flaws.
- Connect these technical explanations back to the research question's focus on fairness and equity.

Act 4: Stakeholder perspectives (3 minutes)

- Present interviews with or portray scenarios about a balanced range of stakeholders:
  - Policymakers discussing potential regulations.
  - Civil liberties advocates raising concerns about discrimination.
  - Public safety or judicial representatives addressing the challenges of bias mitigation.
- Visually juxtapose these different viewpoints.

Act 5: Towards ethical considerations (2–3 minutes)

- Feature an expert or research data suggesting potential solutions and ethical frameworks for addressing algorithmic bias in facial recognition.
- Show examples of on-going research and development in bias detection and mitigation.
- Raise questions about accountability and oversight.

Conclusion: A personal reflection (2 minutes)

- The filmmaker (you) provides a voiceover summarising the key findings and articulating your personal position on the research question, supported by the evidence presented.
- End with a powerful visual or statement that encourages viewers to think critically about the ethical implications of this technology and its impact.
- Roll credits and resources for further information.

5 Additional written content

Provide a few paragraphs that outline your ethical dilemma, how it relates to your chosen career field, a brief explanation of the format of your film (explain visuals, music, sound effects and other techniques used as appropriate) and any essential explanation of your research or other information that was not adequately reflected in the film. Ensure you do not exceed the maximum total amount of time/number of words combined.

6 Appendix

Bibliography/works cited and a copy of the audio transcript.

> **Remember**
>
> Films can incorporate interviews, expert commentary, real-world footage and even animated sequences to explain complex concepts. Visuals, music and any special effects should be intentional choices that enhance your message. These can be thoughtfully leveraged to portray powerful ideas while reducing the number of words needed to convey the message. All visuals, music and any special effects or filming techniques must be explained in an additional written text.

These are just examples to get you started. The best outline for you will depend on the specific requirements of your project format and how you prefer to organise your thoughts.

> ## Learning journal entry
>
> ### Activity
>
> Before you create an initial outline that structures your project, complete the following activities:
>
> - Write out your ethical dilemma in the form of a research question.
> - Identify and list the contexts you researched.
> - Identify and list the stakeholders whose perspectives you researched.
> - Identify and list important information or new understandings from your research (for example, statistic, quote, image, definition).
> - Identify and list the main resources you plan to use.
> - Write out your personal position. Identify what evidence or values contributed to your choosing this position. List the ways your decision might impact you or others.
> - Identify and list any essential structural or stylistic elements appropriate for your chosen format.
>
> Look back to the sections 'Collating your research', 'Analysing your research', and 'Synthesising your research to determine your personal position' in Chapter 6 if necessary.
>
> ### Feedback
>
> Once you have created your outline, share it with your supervisor or peers for feedback. If there is anything about your outline that you are unsure of, seek specific feedback on it.
>
> Possible questions you might ask:
>
> - Is the structure coherent? Does it make sense for my chosen format?
> - Am I forgetting any essential structural or stylistic conventions?
> - Do my ideas seem to flow logically?
> - Have I included all the requirements? (ethical dilemma, career connection, multiple perspectives, different contexts, analysis of research, justification of a personal position, consideration of impact)
> - Have I **balanced** the perspectives?
> - Is there anything that seems irrelevant that should be removed or revised?

Creating an initial draft

Now you are ready to start work on the first draft of your reflective project.

If you are creating a written project, you can simply follow your outline and begin filling in all the missing details. Be sure to use transition words wisely when changing focus or ideas to help your reader follow the logic of your thinking.

If you are creating a visual, audio or audio-visual project, you might begin by creating your script or visual storyboard before you start work on the actual audio or visual product. This will reduce the amount of editing you might need to do on your audio or video files later. You might also begin collecting the images or video clips you plan to use or arrange to include other participants in the case of an interview, podcast or similar format. Consider doing a test run on a section or segment of your audio or video just to be sure you know how to use the technology properly prior to creating the entire project.

> Use this checklist to ensure you have included all the required elements.
>
> **Content:**
> - ✓ Check that your contexts and examples are relevant.
> - ✓ Balance your discussion of the perspectives so that your reflective project is not one-sided.
> - ✓ Demonstrate that you understand the complexities of your dilemma based on your analysis of the research.
> - ✓ Justify your personal position and your reflections on its potential impact.
>
> **Format:**
> - ✓ Confirm that your structure, language and tone match your format, purpose and audience.
> - ✓ Confirm that you have properly used stylistic conventions of your chosen format.
> - ✓ Check that your method for organising your ideas is used consistently and that you have made logical transitions between ideas.
> - ✓ Make sure your communication is clear and concise.
> - ✓ Use a consistent method of citation for ideas from your research that are not your own.
>
> **Reflection:**
> - ✓ Keep track of your reflections on process and feedback in your learning journal as you develop and edit your project.

Remember

If you are not writing a dissertation-style essay, are there any requirements that do not easily fit into your format? Remember that you still have additional words to use to account for anything that's missing. Even if you feel your reflective project includes everything – you should use the additional words to reiterate your ethical dilemma, connect it to your career field, explain why you chose your format, how you approached your project (for example, why you used certain images or structural conventions), how you conducted your research, and restate your personal position.

Citations and referencing

In Chapter 5, you learned how to analyse sources for bias and credibility and how to create an annotated bibliography. Using these sources in the development of your project shows that you have not only carried out relevant research, but also that you have understood it, analysed it, and put it all together to draw conclusions (all of these are important **thinking** skills) and develop your personal position.

When sharing information from your research in your reflective project, including facts, quotations, data, theories, principles and images, it is important to state where this information has come from – that is, to cite the source. Even if you paraphrase information from your research, if the idea was someone else's you need to cite the source. Just as you want credit for your own work, other researchers deserve recognition for theirs.

Acknowledging the contributions and work of others (including the use of AI) is a matter of academic integrity and part of demonstrating a **principled** approach. It also allows readers to check evidence or conduct further research for themselves. Proper referencing and citation are also essential to avoid plagiarism – presenting someone else's work as your own.

Remember

Even if plagiarism is accidental, you could still be penalised for it, so be diligent about citing your sources! If you are not sure whether to cite a source, it is better to cite it to ensure you are always working with the utmost personal and academic integrity.

In-text citations briefly refer to a source within the main body of your writing. This usually includes the author's last name and year of publication, and sometimes a page number. Link the citation to a source listed in your bibliography or works cited page (see examples below).

A reference list provides a detailed list in your reflective project appendix that includes all the bibliographic information for each source cited. The format of entries in the reference list varies depending on the style. This is also sometimes called a 'works cited' page (see the examples below and in Chapter 5).

Example

Below are some examples of the most frequently used citation styles in academic research.

1. **APA (American Psychological Association) style:**
   - Commonly used in social sciences (psychology, education, sociology, business, nursing).
   - In-text citation (parenthetical):
     - One author: (Smith, 2020)
     - Two authors: (Smith & Jones, 2023)
     - Three or more authors: (Smith et al., 2021). Note: that 'et al.' is used after the first author's name.
     - Direct quote: (Smith, 2020, p. 45)
   - Reference list entry (book): Smith, J. (2020). *The impact of social media*. Academic Press.
   - Reference list entry (journal article): Jones, A., & Brown, B. (2023). Exploring new frontiers in AI ethics. *Journal of Artificial Intelligence Research, 15*(2), 112–130.

2. **MLA (Modern Language Association) style:**
   - Commonly used in humanities (literature, languages, cultural studies).
   - In-text citation (parenthetical):
     - One author: (Smith 37)
     - Direct quote: (Jones 102–03)
   - Works cited entry (book): Smith, John. *The Evolving Novel*. University Press, 2022.
   - Works cited entry (journal article): Brown, Emily, and Laura Davis. 'The Representation of Identity in Modern Poetry.' *Journal of Literary Analysis*, vol. 25, no. 1, 2024, pp. 56–72.

3. **Chicago/Turabian style:**
   - Commonly used in history, business and some humanities disciplines. Offers two systems:
     - Notes and bibliography: Uses footnotes or endnotes for citations, with a bibliography at the end.
     - Author-date: Similar to APA, using parenthetical in-text citations and a reference list.
   - Example (Notes and bibliography – footnote): Joel Colton and Lloyd Kramer, *A History of the Modern World* (New York: McGraw-Hill, 2007), 156.
   - Example (Notes and bibliography – bibliography entry – Book): Colton, Joel, and Lloyd Kramer. *A History of the Modern World*. New York: McGraw-Hill, 2007.
   - Example (Author-date – In-text citation): (Colton & Kramer, 2007, 156)
   - Example (Author-date – reference list entry – book): Colton, Joel, and Lloyd Kramer. 2007. *A History of the Modern World*. New York: McGraw-Hill.

As you may have noticed, certain styles are commonly used in particular disciplines. While this might influence which style you choose, there are no rules about this for the reflective project. Choose the style that you are most comfortable with – just make sure you use it consistently throughout.

For online resources, make sure to include the date the article was retrieved as part of your reference list entry.

Footnotes and endnotes are not necessary, but if you decide to use them, you must do so properly, bearing in mind that they are part of the total word count.

Tips for citations

✓ Stay organised: Keep track of your sources from the beginning of your research in your learning journal. Your annotated bibliography can help you record and organise your sources.

✓ Start early and cite as you go: You will be working on your RP for several months, so you should use citations even in drafts – any time you quote or reference your research. That way you will not forget to cite a source, which might then be flagged as plagiarism.

✓ Be consistent: Once you choose a style, pay attention to the specific formatting rules and use them correctly and consistently.

✓ Use a citation management tool: Online tools, such as Zotero, Mendeley and EndNote, can help you organise your sources electronically, and automatically generate citations and reference lists in various styles. Try whatever is easily accessible to you in your word-processing software. You can also ask your school librarian for advice.

✓ Double-check: Before submitting your work, carefully review all your in-text citations and your reference list to ensure accuracy and consistency.

> ## Learning journal entry
>
> ### Activity
>
> Look at some of the sources you used in your research. Note down what methods of citation they used and how they referenced their sources.
>
> ### Reflection
>
> Which method of citation and referencing appeals to you and why?
>
> Do you have access to word-processing tools that can support your ability to cite and reference effectively? Who can help you with this?

Academic integrity

There are several aspects of academic integrity that are essential to the reflective project.

Authenticity: Your work must be your own original creation. While you can receive guidance from your supervisor and others, you need to do the research and writing yourself. You must do your own proofreading of your initial draft, because your reflective project supervisor is only allowed to comment in writing on one draft before you finalise your project and submit it. Even then, they cannot correct your spelling, grammar or formatting.

Proper citation: Readers should be able to easily distinguish between your own work and where you have used others' ideas, by your use of clear citation or footnote indicators. Word-for-word quotations must be signalled with quotation marks or presented as indented paragraphs for lengthy quotes.

Accurate reporting: Readers must also be able to trust that you are reporting your research and findings as fully and accurately as possible. You should never alter facts or manipulate data to fit the outcome you want.

Authenticity is particularly important, not only for the integrity of your work, but also for your own personal integrity. While you are allowed to discuss ideas and to give and receive feedback from your peers, the reflective project should be an individual piece of work – unlike work you may have done in other courses, where collaboration is encouraged and work is assessed as a group effort.

Collusion is a breach of academic integrity, and it happens when learners cooperate or collaborate to complete work that is intended to be submitted for individual assessment. Specifically, for the reflective project you must not:

- allow your work to be submitted as part of someone else's assessment
- include the work of another student as your own
- co-write information for work submitted for assessment either as yours or someone else's.

In Chapter 5 you learned about 'Dos and Don'ts' for using AI as you research and develop your reflective project. Following the rules for using technology is also an important part of academic integrity. Be sure that you are using technology tools in an allowable, responsible, appropriate way. Remember that if AI is used in creating your reflective project, it must be cited or referenced as described in Chapter 5.

Remember

You will put your IB Career-related Programme Certificate at risk if you breach any of the IB regulations on academic integrity or ethical research. If you are unsure or confused about what is allowed and what is not, ask your reflective project supervisor.

Learning journal entry

Reflection

Why is academic integrity always important?

Why is it especially important for the reflective project?

How is it important in your future career?

Reviewing your draft

Once you have completed your first draft, use the following checklist to confirm that you have included all the requirements of the reflective project.

Requirement	What it means
Ethical dilemma	Your ethical dilemma has more than one possible solution, neither of which is without its drawbacks. You make a clear connection between your ethical dilemma and your career field.
Context and perspectives	Contexts: You use clear and relevant examples from multiple appropriate contexts (for example, local, global, historical, economic, political, sociological, environmental, and so on) that help contribute to a comprehensive understanding of the dilemma. Perspectives: You consider the dilemma from different points of view. You approach it in a fair and balanced way, showing the complexity of the issue.
Research	You use a variety of sources to explore different opinions about the dilemma. Your analysis shows that you understood the research and have brought together relevant information and drawn logical conclusions.
Personal position	You show that you have thought critically about the dilemma, the research and different perspectives. Based on this evidence, you decide where you stand on the dilemma. You can explain your position clearly with good reasons based on what you learned by doing your research. You explain how it might impact all the stakeholders if you were making the decision as a professional.
Clear communication	Your ideas are organised so that they flow logically and coherently. Depending on the format of your reflective project (essay, podcast, presentation, and so on) your project is structured using the correct style or conventions that fit your chosen format.
References and citations	You have created a bibliography and chosen a citation method to use consistently throughout your project. You give proper credit to your sources.

Requirement	What it means
Written reflection	You will complete a final written reflection after your final draft, but you can begin now to write reflections and notes in your learning journal that show how you have thought deeply about your research, planning, and process. Record the feedback you receive and the actions you take to improve so that these can make up part of your final written reflection.

Using the assessment criteria to self-evaluate your project

While there are opportunities for peer support and feedback throughout your reflective project journey (for example, choosing your dilemma and format, planning your research methods, confirming that your thinking is on track based on your outline or presentations), your supervisor can only comment on one version of your draft project. So, it makes sense to have your supervisor give you specific, detailed feedback on the second draft you create following your presentation of findings. While you can ask for general feedback and support from your supervisor or peers, a great way to ensure you are on track is by using the assessment criteria to evaluate the first draft of your project yourself. You will also want to do this later, for your final version.

Criterion A: Focus on the ethical dilemma

This criterion looks at how well you identify an ethical dilemma connected to a career field and how deeply you explore it through different perspectives and contexts.

Questions to ask yourself:

- Have I related my ethical dilemma to a career I am interested in?
- Have I looked at the ethical dilemma from several different angles?
- Am I keeping my focus on the dilemma with good examples from different situations?

Example

Here are some examples of what you could do, using an ethical dilemma from the field of healthcare about whether to provide limited resources to treat a patient with a low chance of survival when it could save another patient with a higher chance.

	What excellent achievement looks like	Tips for aiming high	Examples of what you can do
Nature of the ethical dilemma	Your ethical dilemma is clearly and precisely defined. It could lead to several possible resolutions.	Make sure your research question and introduction clearly explain the ethical dilemma.	Frame your research question to outline the ethical dilemma, for example 'Should healthcare providers give limited medical resources to a patient with a low chance of survival, or instead allocate these resources to save another patient with a higher chance of survival?'

	What excellent achievement looks like	Tips for aiming high	Examples of what you can do
	You clearly explain how this dilemma connects to a specific career.	Explain why this dilemma matters for the career you are interested in and why it is important to others working in that field. Talk about how this dilemma affects people, communities, and society as a whole. Show that there is not just one 'right' answer –there could be many solutions depending on different values or viewpoints.	State that as an aspiring healthcare professional, you might face tough decisions about how to allocate scarce medical resources. This dilemma is highly relevant because your future career will involve making challenging choices that affect patients' lives. The way you approach this issue has significant implications for individual patients, healthcare organisations and the broader community. It is a critical ethical consideration that all practitioners in the healthcare field must be prepared to navigate. Explain that this dilemma raises questions of fairness, equity and the ethical obligation to maximise positive outcomes, indicating that there is no universally 'right' answer; different resolutions may be justified based on various ethical frameworks.
Perspectives	You explore different viewpoints on the dilemma fairly and thoroughly, giving each a balanced evaluation.	Identify who is affected by the dilemma and explore their different opinions and values. Give each perspective appropriate and equal attention, so you can dig into the reasons and consequences behind each one. Recognise that the dilemma is complex and that solutions might change depending on the situation and the people involved.	Identify key stakeholders impacted by the ethical dilemma, including patients, their families, healthcare providers, healthcare organisations, policymakers and the broader community. Explore the differing perspectives of these stakeholders, such as patients' desire for treatment, healthcare providers' ethical obligations, the organisation's financial constraints, and community concerns about fairness and equitable access to healthcare. Recognise that various factors, including patients' personal circumstances, professional ethics of healthcare providers, organisational policies, and community expectations, all contribute to the complexity of this issue and the various possible outcomes.
Focus and context	You keep a clear and steady focus on the ethical dilemma throughout your project.	Keep your project focused on the ethical dilemma – make sure everything you discuss connects back to it. Use clear examples or case studies from different contexts to show how the dilemma plays out in real life. Discuss how the context changes how people understand and deal with the dilemma.	Maintain a clear focus on the ethical dilemma throughout your project. Show how the dilemma can manifest differently in various healthcare contexts, such as: o a rural hospital with limited resources facing this decision o a large urban academic medical centre with more advanced treatment options o a paediatric hospital treating children with rare, life-threatening conditions o a government-run universal healthcare system grappling with resource allocation

	What excellent achievement looks like	Tips for aiming high	Examples of what you can do
			Consider how resource constraints, patient demographics, organisational policies and community expectations can lead to different considerations and potential resolutions in each context. Additionally, the socioeconomic status of the patients, the availability of alternative treatment options and the public's perception of the healthcare system can all influence the ethical implications. Understanding the context-specific factors is essential for a comprehensive evaluation of the dilemma. However, be mindful not to delve too deeply into any one context, as this could disrupt the overall balance of your analysis.

Criterion B: Knowledge and understanding through research

This criterion assesses how well you use research to deepen your understanding of the ethical dilemma and its effects.

Questions to ask yourself:

- Have I done my research thoroughly and effectively?
- Do I understand the issues connected to the ethical dilemma?
- Have I thought about how the ethical dilemma affects people or groups in different situations?

Example

Here are some examples of what you could do, using an ethical dilemma about whether a factory development plan has a negative impact on its neighbouring environment.

	What excellent achievement looks like	Tips for aiming high	Examples of what you can do
Research	Your research covers a wide range of sources and goes deep into the topic. You use many different resources to get a full picture.	Plan your research carefully and use a variety of reliable sources. Check each source for biases, especially when it is important for your analysis. Make sure your research looks at many sides of the ethical dilemma.	Investigate scientific studies that focus on the environmental impacts of factory developments, such as air and water pollution levels in nearby communities and on local wildlife. Review government policies and regulations related to environmental protection. Explore economic factors and implications, such as potential job creation, infrastructure improvements and tax revenue for the local community. Review public health studies that reveal the perceived complications associated with industrial development in residential areas.

	What excellent achievement looks like	Tips for aiming high	Examples of what you can do
		Think about how the dilemma plays out in different contexts – under different social, economic and cultural settings – and how it affects different people or groups. Organise your research so it shows both the big picture and the details. This will help you build a strong analysis later.	Conduct interviews with a diverse group of stakeholders, such as urban planners, conservation experts, factory plan developers and local residents to gather first-hand perspectives related to this dilemma. Look into different media outlets and their covered stories on this topic. You can also explore case studies of similar factory developments in other regions or areas to understand both the positive and negative consequences that occurred.
Knowledge and understanding	Your project demonstrates that you really know and understand the issues connected to your ethical dilemma.	Use your research to clearly explain the main issues and concerns related to your ethical dilemma, showing that you understand the topic deeply and in detail. If it fits, connect your findings to ethical theories or principles. These frameworks can help explain your understanding, but do not let them overshadow the unique details of your ethical dilemma.	Focus on the trade-offs between economic growth and environmental preservation. Discuss scientific evidence on potential ecological consequences alongside the socioeconomic implications for the local community. Incorporate concepts from environmental economics, such as the idea of 'precautionary principle' to discuss ethical considerations. You might also link to ethical theories like utilitarianism and deontology as they relate to environmental and sustainability ethics.
Impact of dilemma	You clearly explain how different people, groups or situations are affected by the dilemma, showing a strong understanding of its impact.	Identify who the key stakeholders are – the people, communities or environments affected by the ethical dilemma. Analyse how these groups are impacted, in both good and bad ways. Show that you understand the different interests and concerns of each group, including any trade-offs they might face.	Explore how the factory development might affect local residents' livelihoods, the wellbeing of wildlife and the long-term sustainability of the region's ecosystem. Investigate how the factory development might impact various individuals or groups, perhaps relating to the stakeholder groups you identified earlier. For example: • local residents may welcome the potential for new job opportunities and improved infrastructure but others may be concerned about the environmental impact and disruption to their daily lives • environment advocacy groups may be strongly against the development plan • local business owners may see the factory as an opportunity for economic growth and profitability • policymakers may be torn between the potential benefits and their responsibility to protect the public good

	What excellent achievement looks like	Tips for aiming high	Examples of what you can do
		Place your ethical dilemma within the bigger social, economic, political or environmental contexts. Discuss possible solutions or ideas to reduce any negative effects.	• factory employees may welcome the new job opportunities, however they may worry about workplace safety, labour rights and long-term job security • younger generations might also be affected by the long-term impacts of the factory development.

Criterion C: Critical thinking

This criterion looks at how well you have analysed your research and put it all together to form and explain your own position on the ethical dilemma. It also checks if you have thought about how your position might affect different people and situations.

Questions to ask yourself:

- Have I carefully analysed and combined my research?
- Have I clearly decided where I stand on the ethical dilemma?
- Have I explained and supported my position with good reasons?
- Have I thought about how my position might impact others?

Example

Here are some examples of what you could do, using an ethical dilemma regarding whether the pursuit of winning in sports takes priority over athletes' wellbeing.

	What excellent achievement looks like	Tips for aiming high	Examples of what you can do
Analysis and synthesis of research	You have thoroughly analysed and combined your research. You discuss important findings clearly and effectively.	Dive deep into your research and analyse it, carefully. Look at different viewpoints, data and information. Bring your research together by identifying key themes, patterns and connections between your sources. Present your findings clearly and logically, so your ideas make sense and are easy to follow.	Analyse research on the physical, mental and emotional effects the pursuit of winning has on athletes, considering both positive and negative aspects. Synthesise findings from various scientific research, case studies, athlete testimonials and expert interviews to identify the key tensions and trade-offs between the drive to win and the prioritisation of athlete wellbeing. Research policies and changes of policy based on research and case studies – for example, the use of helmets in American football and the NFL policy on removal of players who are deemed to be concussed.

	What excellent achievement looks like	Tips for aiming high	Examples of what you can do
		Use your research to build a strong, well-informed understanding of the dilemma, helping you make smart decisions and suggestions.	Include an analysis of the various stakeholders involved (athletes, coaches, sports organisations, fans) and how their competing interests and perspectives shape the ethical landscape. It could also incorporate relevant ethical frameworks, such as the duty of care and the principle of beneficence, to provide a nuanced understanding of the issue.
			Demonstrate a deep understanding of the issue by exploring the broader societal and cultural factors that contribute to the prioritisation of winning in sports, such as the commercialisation of sports, the pressure for national and organisational success, and the glorification of athletic achievement. The analysis could consider the contrasting and differing perspectives under different cultural and contextual factors, such as gender, religion, race, class, ethnicity, age, education, political affiliation and history.
Personal position: reasoning and evidence	You clearly state your personal position. Your position is backed up by strong, well-focused reasoning linked to carefully chosen evidence.	Clearly say what your personal position is on the ethical dilemma. Support your position with solid arguments based on your research. Make sure there is a clear link between what you say and the evidence you found.	Based on thorough research and analysis, propose well-informed recommendations or solutions to strike a better balance between the pursuit of winning and prioritising athlete wellbeing.
			These recommendations could include policy changes within sports organisations, enhanced mental health support for athletes, improved coach education and accountability, and the implementation of clear guidelines and regulations to protect athlete welfare.
			Suggest areas for further research, cross-collaboration between sports, medicine and psychology and the inclusion of athlete voices in decision-making processes.
Personal position: justification and impact	You provide a clear and convincing explanation for your position. You show that you have seriously thought about how your position might affect different people or groups.	Explain why your position makes sense and why it matters. Think about how your position might affect different people or groups – both the good and the bad sides. Show that you have carefully considered the possible consequences of your position in different contexts.	Justify your position by acknowledging the complex, multifaceted nature of the ethical dilemma. For example, while the pursuit of winning is essential in competitive sports, prioritising it above all can have detrimental consequences for athletes' physical and mental health. Conversely, the drive to excel fosters positive attributes such as determination and resilience. A balanced approach allows athletes to thrive in competition while maintaining overall wellbeing. However, this balance requires careful consideration and a firm stance. A well-supported argument must ultimately advocate for a clear prioritisation, even if that is with its own inherent challenges. Acknowledging the complexities and potential drawbacks of that position only strengthens

	What excellent achievement looks like	Tips for aiming high	Examples of what you can do
			the argument, demonstrating a comprehensive understanding of the ethical dilemma. Potential consequences of your personal position might be that: • athletes might enjoy longer, more sustainable careers and a healthier relationship with their sport • coaches and sports organisations may need to change training regimens and performance metrics, shifting from a sole focus on winning to a more holistic understanding of sports' value for individual and community development • fans and other community members' experiences could also be enhanced, fostering a deeper appreciation for the athlete's journey and sportspersonship.

Criterion D: Communication of ideas

This criterion looks at how well you organise your ideas and use the right language and structure to share your thoughts clearly and effectively.

Questions to ask yourself:

- Have I used the right terms and structure to explain my ideas in the best way possible?
- Are my ideas easy to follow and well organised so people understand me clearly?

Example

Here are some examples of what you could do, using an ethical dilemma regarding whether the use of human germline editing should be allowed to prevent inherited diseases.

	What excellent achievement looks like	Tips for aiming high	Examples of what you can do
Terminology	You use relevant terms and style choices consistently and correctly to help get your ideas across.	Use the important terms and language from your research and topic to explain your ideas clearly and accurately. Keep using these terms consistently throughout your project to make your points clear and connected. Make smart style choices like tone, voice, formatting, visuals or music that fit your project type and audience. These should make your message stronger and easier to understand.	Incorporate specific topic-related terms like 'gene editing', 'informed consent', 'bioethics' and 'genetic privacy' accurately and consistently. However, avoid jargon or overly technical language that could confuse the reader. If you choose to do this topic as a business proposal on somatic gene therapy development as an alternative to germline editing, ensure that you stick to an appropriate structure, formatting and tone for a business proposal setting. If your chosen format is a formal speech at a medical conference, tailor the language, tone and message to be appropriate for your targeted audience and setting. You might use rhetorical devices such as questions, quotations or anecdotes to engage the audience.

	What excellent achievement looks like	Tips for aiming high	Examples of what you can do
Structure	Your project is organised in a way that makes your ideas clear and easy to follow.	Organise your project so your audience can easily follow your thinking from start to finish. Use headings, subheadings, labels (for graphs or tables), transitions, bullet points, quotations and other tools to help organise your work. Present your ideas in a logical order, making sure each part flows smoothly into the next to keep your story connected. Stick to the structure that fits your chosen format (like essay, podcast, presentation), and make sure you have a strong beginning and ending to wrap things up clearly.	Use sections such as 'Introduction', 'Research plan', 'Nature of the identified ethical dilemma', 'Stakeholder perspectives', 'Research findings', 'Analysis and synthesis', 'Personal position', 'Justification', 'Impact and conclusion'. This structure aids the audience in understanding the progression and development of your ideas.
Development and organisation of ideas	Your ideas are well explained and presented in a logical, easy-to-understand manner.	Develop your ideas fully, giving enough detail and evidence to explore the ethical dilemma carefully. Make sure your ideas connect well, showing clear links between different parts of your analysis. Use transitions to help your audience move smoothly from one section to the next, making it easy to follow your argument. Let your research findings naturally lead into your personal position, which should be clearly supported and explained using evidence from your research.	When discussing the impact of the ethical dilemma, provide detailed examples of how similar situations have been addressed in other contexts, influenced by different cultural factors, drawing parallels to your case. Use transitions to smoothly shift between different aspects of your argument. For example, to build on an idea you can use expressions such as 'Building on this point', 'Furthermore'. To move from discussing negative impacts to highlighting positive influences you can use expressions such as 'Conversely' or 'In contrast'. To draw a conclusion, you can use expressions such as 'As a result'. In discussing the impact of human germline editing, you might first outline the potential benefits, then transition to potential risks, and finally present your recommendations for responsible development and use. This logical progression helps your audience grasp the complexities of the ethical dilemma and understand the rationale behind your conclusions.

Criterion E: Reflective practice

This criterion looks at how well you show that you have thought about and learned from your project as you planned, researched and completed it.

Questions to ask yourself:

- Have I demonstrated reflective practice?
- Have I reflected on my learning and the choices I made?
- Have I thought about how this project has affected me and might affect others?
- Have I critically looked at my own and others' ideas, actions or decisions?

Example

Here are some examples of what you could do.

	What excellent achievement looks like	Tips for aiming high	Examples of what you can do
Reflection on process	Your reflections explain your decisions, actions and thinking clearly, and most of them are well justified.	Explain important decisions you made while planning, researching and developing your project. Talk about how these choices shaped your thinking and approach. Reflect on any feedback you got during the process. Explain whether you acted on it or not, why you made those choices, and how they affected your project. Talk about any challenges you faced and how you dealt with them. Share what you learned from these experiences and how it might help you in future learning or projects.	Reflect on your ability to gather and interpret data, identify key issues and apply ethical frameworks. You might want to elaborate on which strategies were effective, and which may need improvement. For example, you could discuss how you initially relied on scholarly articles and interviews with experts as your main data sources but found them to be somewhat one-sided. After taking feedback from your supervisor, you sought out diverse case studies that offered more nuanced insights. Reflect on challenges you encountered in accessing certain sources or navigating ethical considerations related to your research. For example, you might describe how you sought support from teachers and school librarians, who helped you find diverse perspectives related to the ethical issue. Discuss how your approach or your proposed solution could impact professionals in your career field or benefit other stakeholders related to your ethical dilemma.
Reflection on project	You give a detailed evaluation of how well your project worked. You explain what worked well and what did not.	Think about how your understanding of the topic changed as you worked on your project. Reflect on how your **knowledge** and skill grew. Look back at the goals you set at the start and evaluate how well you met them.	You could describe how your initial views on the ethical dilemma changed as you engaged with diverse viewpoints and research findings. You might want to consider discussing specific milestones, such as completing the research phase or drafting plans, and how supervisor meetings and peer feedback influenced your overall learning and decision-making.

	What excellent achievement looks like	Tips for aiming high	Examples of what you can do
		Highlight the strengths of your project and why you think it was successful. Reflect on what you might do differently if you could do the project again, or how you would approach similar projects in the future.	You might want to reflect on how far you have come, what you have accomplished, and whether you have met your intended goals or objectives. You could also evaluate the effectiveness of your overall approach and what you might have done differently in hindsight.
Reflection on learning	You thoroughly discuss how your learning and new understandings have impacted you and others.	Identify the main lessons you learned from your research and reflection. Discuss how the project has changed or influenced your view of the ethical dilemma. Think about how you can use what you have learned in future classes, projects, or in real life.	You might want to highlight insights such as the complexity of the ethical decision-making process and the importance of considering diverse stakeholder perspectives. You could explain how the project has shaped your view on the necessity of ethical guidelines in your future practice and career, and how this awareness will guide your future work. You could consider how the skills and knowledge gained through this process can be applied in your future academic endeavours or career paths. You could consider how the increased understanding of this ethical dilemma could influence the public discourse and policymaking related to the issue. Discuss how this might lead to a more informed public, leading to changes in societal attitudes, regulations or resource allocation.

Feedback and revision

Remember that a first draft is not your final project. You should expect to edit your project and make revisions based on feedback or further thinking.

The reflective project is an independent task and a formal assessment component of the Career-related Programme. Therefore, you cannot receive assistance with any aspect of the research, writing or proofreading of the project beyond that which is permitted through your reflective project supervisor.

When edits or revisions are needed, use word-processing tools to track changes and document different versions of your project. This is also useful for documenting authenticity which is important for academic integrity.

Learning journal entry

Activity

Use the checklist and criteria to evaluate your first draft.

Reflection

How did your ideas flow?

Was there anything you left out?

Was your project structured in a way that reflects the format you chose?

What marks did you give yourself?

What questions or concerns emerged?

Feedback

How will you use the feedback from this activity and from your supervisor?

What did you learn about your essay's organisation? Your content?

What changes will you make based on this activity?

How might this help with your final project?

Key takeaways: Chapter 7

- You can choose from a variety of formats to create your reflective project.
- Different formats have different structural and stylistic elements, so make sure you are familiar with these before developing your project.
- A detailed outline is an effective way to prepare for developing your first draft.
- When creating your first draft, be sure to include all required elements.
- Effective citation and referencing are critical to maintaining academic integrity.
- You can use the criteria to support the development and editing of your project.

Key terms

abstract: a summary of the contents of a piece of academic research

anecdote: a short, sometimes amusing, account of something that has happened

call to action: an exhortation to do something to achieve an aim or deal with a problem

dialogue tagging: also known as speech tags, these are phrases that are used to break up sections of written dialogue (for example, 'he said')

diction: choice of words or the manner of expression

dissertation: a long essay on a particular subject

executive summary: a written account that gives an overview of the main points in a longer document, such as a report or plan

expository essay: an essay that aims to inform a reader about something, or to explain something to them

footage: the extent of film material that has been shot

paraphrase: to express what someone else has written or said using your own words

point of view: a mental viewpoint or attitude

segment: sections of film or television footage that each focus on a particular thing

syntax: the way that words are put together to make sentences

tone: the general attitude or feeling of a piece of writing

transition: word or phrase that indicates the relationship between ideas in a piece of writing

voiceover: a piece of narration in a film or television piece, where the speaker does not appear on camera

Chapter 8 – Presenting your findings

This chapter covers the following:
- The purpose and content of the presentation
- Planning your presentation
- Using communication skills effectively to present your findings
- Using feedback to improve your final draft

Learner profile traits

Knowledgeable

Thinkers

Communicators

Open-minded

Balanced

Reflective

The purpose and content of the presentation

Now that you have created an outline and initial draft of your project, you will present your findings to others before going further. This gives you the chance to explain your process and thinking to others, receive feedback, and improve your project.

You will prepare a short presentation (no more than 10 minutes) based on your research and first draft of your project. Depending on your school, your audience may be made up of peers, supervisors, a panel of teachers, family members or other appropriate members of the wider school community.

The purpose of the reflective project presentation is to practise your **communication** skills, share what you have learned, and receive feedback. For your peers and other school community members, the presentation is a chance to learn about your ethical dilemma, your research and the impact your learning has made on your **thinking**. Teachers and supervisors can also see your progress and check that you are heading in the right direction. Most importantly, you can clarify your thinking, **reflect** on any feedback, and improve your project before finalising and submitting it.

While there is not a specific format required for your presentation, you should include the following information.

Your presentation should include:

- ✓ your research question/ethical dilemma and how it relates to your career field
- ✓ a description of the contexts and perspectives you explored
- ✓ an outline of your research (what your methodology was, any key resources)
- ✓ the results of your research findings (what you learned when you analysed your research)
- ✓ whether and how your thinking, understanding or **knowledge** changed because of your research
- ✓ your personal position on the dilemma (how you arrived at your personal position and how your position might have an impact on others if you were an actual career practitioner)
- ✓ how your learning and new understandings might have an impact on your future education or career.

Remember

If you use your outline and first draft to prepare for your presentation, everything on the checklist should already be there, so check that you have considered all these ideas in your project. If you use presentation software (such as PowerPoint, Prezi, Google Slides, Sway, and so on) you can create one slide for each of the required items as an additional way of checking that you have included everything.

Planning your presentation

While your teacher might give you some specific expectations, there is no mandatory format for the presentation, and it is not assessed by the IB. You can use any type of presentation software, visuals or supplemental materials you want. The presentation is relatively short – up to 10 minutes – but there may be a question-and-answer period at the end.

Preparation is an important part of success, so consider the suggestions below to help you plan out your presentation.

Remember

You have done the research, created your rough draft, and you have your learning journal entries – use all of these as the starting point for your planning.

Organisation

Structure your presentation so that you can present all the required information effectively within your 10-minute timeframe – it goes faster than you think! Here are some tips for planning your presentation.

Create an outline: Plan the key points you want to share, just like you did to prepare for your first draft. Break down your presentation into logical sections based on the content you are sharing.

Decide timings for each section: Determine roughly how much time you want to spend on each section, then adjust your content to fit into your timeframe. For example, the introduction of your ethical dilemma will probably be short, but you might want to spend more time justifying your personal position. If you have several different perspectives, consider how to address them all. Some might only have a brief mention while others need more explanation. Or perhaps you can group stakeholder perspectives to ensure all are addressed in a **balanced** way.

Make notes: When creating slides or speaking notes, do not write out every single word like a script. Instead, jot down the main ideas you want to cover for each part of your presentation. This will help you sound more natural and less like you are reading. If you have slides, use key words or images as memory prompts to help you speak without relying too heavily on notes.

Plan for the Q&A: Be prepared for any questions by reviewing and understanding your project. But remember – you are the expert! You know what you did, why you did it and what you learned. You are sharing your project, but more importantly, you are sharing your personal journey through the project. What were your challenges? What surprised you? What are you most proud of?

Delivery

If your presentation is not effective, the strength of your ideas can be lost on your audience. The tips below will help you present your ideas in an engaging way.

Start strong: Grab your audience's attention right away by starting with a hook. You could share a surprising fact you learned, ask a thought-provoking rhetorical question related to your dilemma or tell a brief, interesting story about your experience.

Show and tell: Visuals are your friend! You can share images, graphs or even a very short video clip if appropriate. But if you are using slides, limit them to key words – they should *support* what you are saying, not *be* what you saying. Keep them clean, brief and easy to read.

Identify personal cues in advance: Have a subtle way to keep track of time during your presentation. While you can use a watch or a timer (with no sound) during your presentation, you might also want to insert a certain image, bullet point or slide as your cue for how far along you are in your presentation. You can also ask a peer or teacher to give you a visual cue at your half-way point – this will help you know whether you should adjust your presentation by speeding up or slowing down.

Strike the right tone: Imagine you are explaining your project to a friend or peer who is genuinely interested. Use a friendly and conversational tone. Your own enthusiasm for your project will be contagious and keep your audience interested.

Use transitions: Use transition words and phrases (both verbally and visually if you have slides) to guide your audience from one point to the next.

Wrap up: Your conclusion should summarise your position and your project and leave your audience with a clear understanding of what you have achieved and learned.

Practice

As the saying goes: practice makes perfect! Even if you are a confident presenter, it is important to practise so that you can be sure your presentation fits into the time allowed and that you know exactly what you want to say. Run through your presentation multiple times to ensure a smooth delivery and to build confidence. You can practise in front of a mirror, with a peer who times you or gives feedback, or with a parent or friend who records you so you can watch it back. This will help you to identify areas for improvement and refine your presentation and timing, so that you do not end up off task or speak too quickly and rush your presentation – or have an awkward silence – during the real thing.

> **Learning journal entry**
>
> **Activity**
>
> Create an outline of key points for your presentation.
>
> - How will you structure your presentation?
> - What visual aids or technology tools will you use?
> - What questions do you anticipate from your audience?

Using communication skills effectively to present your findings

For the presentation, you will need to use a variety of communication skills. You will have been using skills of written communication all the way throughout your reflective project journey – recording things in your learning journal, taking notes during your research, creating a bibliography, developing an outline, and so on. Even if you have chosen a non-written format for your project, you will still be doing some writing for your script, annotations and explanations. You will also have been using interpersonal communication skills to work with your peers and supervisor.

The presentation is a chance to use a different set of communication skills. The following sections explore some of the main skills that will help you deliver your presentation confidently and successfully.

Verbal communication

Verbal communication is not just what you say but also how you say it. To make sure your audience can understand you, try to focus on the following speaking skills.

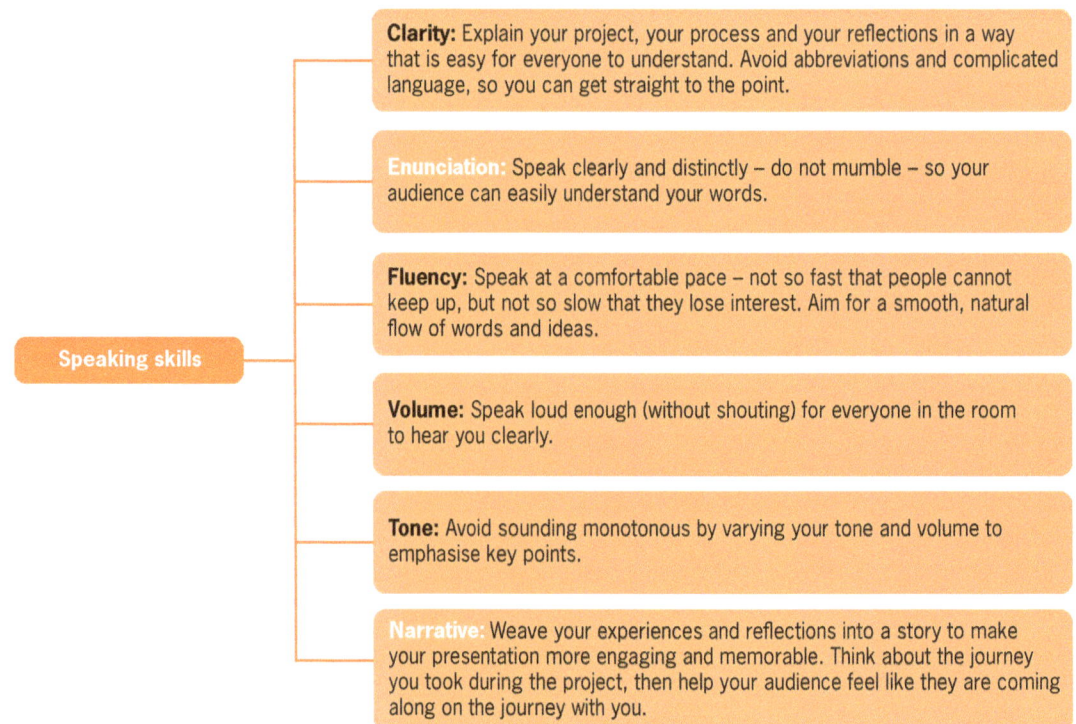

Speaking skills

- **Clarity:** Explain your project, your process and your reflections in a way that is easy for everyone to understand. Avoid abbreviations and complicated language, so you can get straight to the point.
- **Enunciation:** Speak clearly and distinctly – do not mumble – so your audience can easily understand your words.
- **Fluency:** Speak at a comfortable pace – not so fast that people cannot keep up, but not so slow that they lose interest. Aim for a smooth, natural flow of words and ideas.
- **Volume:** Speak loud enough (without shouting) for everyone in the room to hear you clearly.
- **Tone:** Avoid sounding monotonous by varying your tone and volume to emphasise key points.
- **Narrative:** Weave your experiences and reflections into a story to make your presentation more engaging and memorable. Think about the journey you took during the project, then help your audience feel like they are coming along on the journey with you.

Non-verbal communication

Non-verbal communication, or body language, is what you say without using words. When giving a presentation, these non-verbal signals are an important way of letting your audience know you are also interested and engaged in what you are saying.

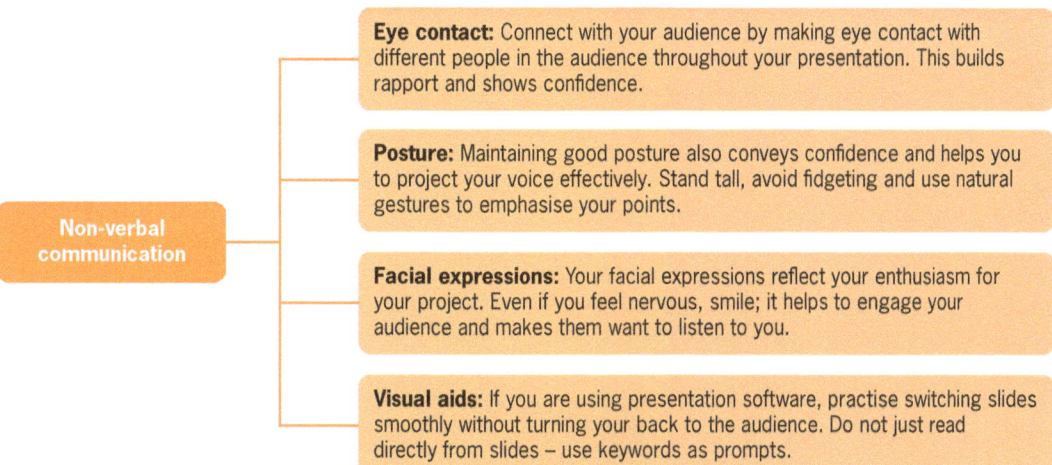

Non-verbal communication

- **Eye contact:** Connect with your audience by making eye contact with different people in the audience throughout your presentation. This builds rapport and shows confidence.
- **Posture:** Maintaining good posture also conveys confidence and helps you to project your voice effectively. Stand tall, avoid fidgeting and use natural gestures to emphasise your points.
- **Facial expressions:** Your facial expressions reflect your enthusiasm for your project. Even if you feel nervous, smile; it helps to engage your audience and makes them want to listen to you.
- **Visual aids:** If you are using presentation software, practise switching slides smoothly without turning your back to the audience. Do not just read directly from slides – use keywords as prompts.

Interpersonal communication

Interpersonal communication focuses on how you connect with others. In a meeting with your supervisor, communication is two-way – you are talking back and forth. A presentation is more one-way because you are doing the talking, but you can engage with your audience in other ways.

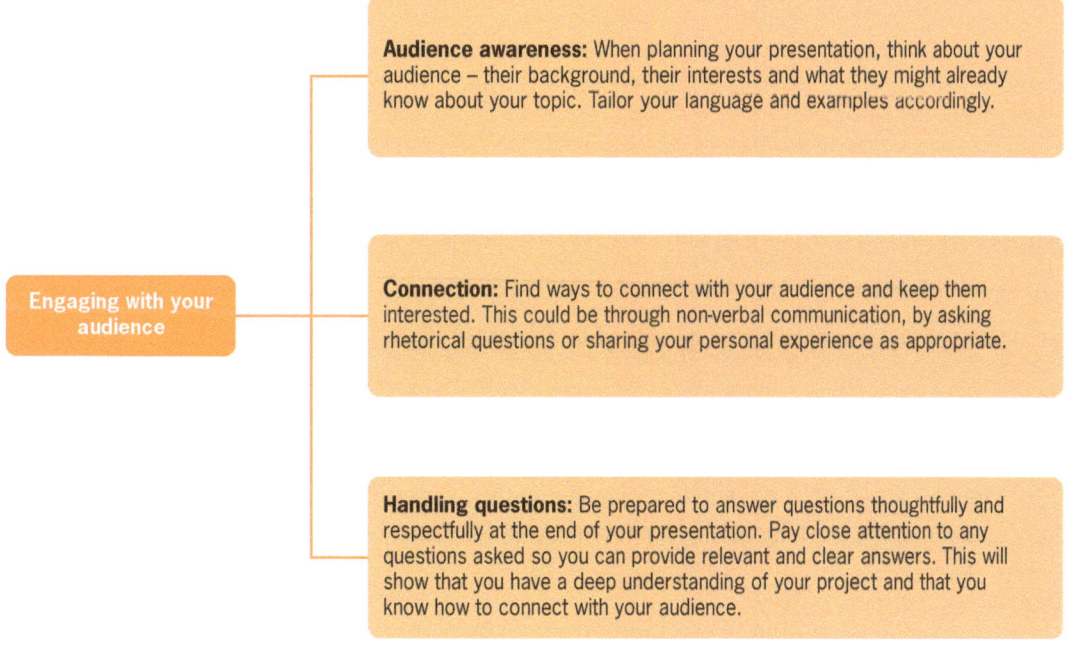

Engaging with your audience

- **Audience awareness:** When planning your presentation, think about your audience – their background, their interests and what they might already know about your topic. Tailor your language and examples accordingly.
- **Connection:** Find ways to connect with your audience and keep them interested. This could be through non-verbal communication, by asking rhetorical questions or sharing your personal experience as appropriate.
- **Handling questions:** Be prepared to answer questions thoughtfully and respectfully at the end of your presentation. Pay close attention to any questions asked so you can provide relevant and clear answers. This will show that you have a deep understanding of your project and that you know how to connect with your audience.

Dealing with nerves

Nerves can happen to everyone – even professional speakers! Try some of the following strategies to help you calm your nerves, or at least not to *appear* nervous to your audience.

How to tackle nerves

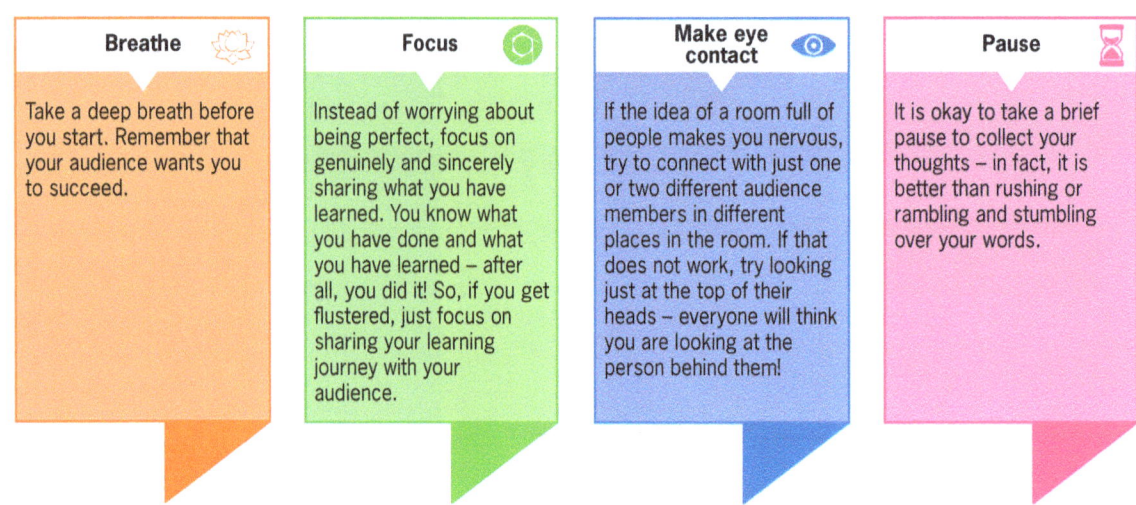

Breathe	Focus	Make eye contact	Pause
Take a deep breath before you start. Remember that your audience wants you to succeed.	Instead of worrying about being perfect, focus on genuinely and sincerely sharing what you have learned. You know what you have done and what you have learned – after all, you did it! So, if you get flustered, just focus on sharing your learning journey with your audience.	If the idea of a room full of people makes you nervous, try to connect with just one or two different audience members in different places in the room. If that does not work, try looking just at the top of their heads – everyone will think you are looking at the person behind them!	It is okay to take a brief pause to collect your thoughts – in fact, it is better than rushing or rambling and stumbling over your words.

Remember

You have already put in the hard work for your reflective project, so this is your chance to share it with others. By honing your communication skills, you will be well-equipped, not just to deliver a compelling and engaging presentation about your reflective project, but for future presentations in other classes or in your career. Be confident, be yourself – and let your passion for your topic shine through!

Learning journal entry

Reflection

Which communication skills do you think are your strongest? Why?

Which needs more practice or improvement to feel prepared for your presentation?

What strategies will you use to engage with your audience?

Activity

You will want to seek feedback about your presentation from your peers and other audience members. Design a feedback survey or questionnaire based on the assessment criteria and share it with your audience, and engage them by asking them to provide feedback on your presentation.

Using feedback to improve your final draft

After the presentation, you should reflect on the status of your current draft and use any feedback provided by your supervisor or peers to decide how to finalise your project. The presentation is the first chance you will have to really *articulate* your thinking and share your research, so you may find that afterwards, your ideas might have changed. For example, if you were not convinced about your personal position, having to explain it to other people, being questioned about it, and receiving feedback might clarify your direction and get you thinking about it in a different way.

It is important to be **open-minded** about any feedback you receive. The presentation is a great opportunity to seek out and take on board ideas on all the ways in which you might be able to improve not only your reflective project but also your communication skills. Ask for feedback on the factors that will be assessed when you submit your final project, such as:

- your analysis of research and contextualisation of the ethical dilemma
- whether your perspectives are well balanced
- how you demonstrated knowledge and understanding of the complexities of your dilemma
- how well you justify your personal position
- how well you explore the impact of the dilemma and your position
- how effectively you organise your thinking
- the clarity and coherence of your argument as you communicate your ideas.

Compare the feedback you receive to the reflective project criteria and decide what actions you can take to improve your project before submitting it. Then, go back to the descriptors (see 'Using the assessment criteria to self-evaluate your project' in Chapter 7) and plan any improvements from there.

Learning journal entry

Feedback

What were the strong points of your presentation?

Did you receive any feedback that you could action to improve your project?

Based on feedback, what aspects of your project might need further development or improvement?

Reflection

What insights have you gained about your project?

Do you need to research anything further? Is any additional analysis needed?

What is your strategy for finalising your project?

Remember

Reflections on feedback and any actions taken should be recorded in your learning journal.

Key takeaways: Chapter 8

- The reflective project presentation is an opportunity to practise communication skills and to share your research and understanding of your ethical dilemma.
- While there is not a mandatory presentation style, there are requirements for the information you should include in your presentation.
- Use the feedback from your presentation to improve your project as you finalise it.

Key terms

articulate: to express or explain your ideas, thoughts or reasoning in a clear, distinct way

enunciation: the act of pronouncing words or parts of words clearly

narrative: an account, report or story of events or experiences

Chapter 9 – Completion and submission

This chapter covers the following:
- Refining your reflective project
- Editing your reflective project
- Evaluating and finalising your reflective project
- Completing and submitting your written reflection
- Preparing for and participating in your viva voce
- Authenticating your work

Learner profile traits

Knowledgeable

Thinkers

Communicators

Open-minded

Balanced

Reflective

Refining your reflective project

In this final phase, you will have two chances to refine your project. Based on the feedback you received from your presentation, you can identify aspects of your project that need further development or revision. **Reflect** on and use the feedback to create a more refined version of your project and to finish up any production tasks if you are creating a non-written format. This refined version is the one you will submit to your supervisor, and is the only draft that they are allowed to comment on.

Once your supervisor provides their feedback, you will have one more chance to make refinements before submitting your project. Make sure that you and your supervisor have set a timeline for the review of your draft so you have time to revise and complete your project before the submission deadline. If there is anything specific about your project that you want feedback on, be sure to let your supervisor know when you give them the draft to review.

Editing your reflective project

Your supervisor is likely to provide feedback in the form of questions or general suggestions, but they cannot edit your work themselves. Once you receive the feedback, make sure you understand what your supervisor is suggesting – ask for clarification if you need to. You learned about the importance of receiving and responding to feedback in Chapters 2 and 8. Hopefully you have been using those ideas throughout your reflective project learning journey, listening to suggestions and guidance and considering it with an **open mind**.

Editing your reflective project – proofreading and checking grammar, content, organisation of ideas, stylistic conventions and quality of audio/audio-visual products – is *your* responsibility. You do not have to implement all feedback, but you should at least consider it carefully to decide whether it would improve your project. Consider any suggested changes, ensure that all necessary elements have been addressed, and create the final version of your reflective project.

Remember

While supervisors will read and comment on your draft project, it is important to remember that they are not allowed to:

- ✗ correct spelling or punctuation errors
- ✗ make decisions or corrections on the format
- ✗ correct information, data or statistics
- ✗ rewrite or reproduce any part of your project
- ✗ indicate where whole sections of text might be rearranged
- ✗ correct bibliographies or citations.

Learning journal entry

Feedback

Which aspects of your project are strongest?
Which areas need improvement?
Does the feedback you have received indicate a need for further revisions? If so, how do you plan to address these?

Evaluating and finalising your reflective project

You saw in Chapter 7 how to use the assessment criteria to develop your reflective project. Now you need to refer to the criteria one more time – to self-evaluate your final project. If anything has been left out or falls in the lower mark bands, adjust it before submission to increase your chances of success. Self-evaluation will reassure you that your project is the best that it can be. It will also help with your final written reflection and in preparing for the viva voce – the final interview with your supervisor.

Your final reflective project should:

- ✓ demonstrate effective research skills
- ✓ indicate a well-focused and appropriate ethical dilemma in the form of a research question
- ✓ contextualise an ethical dilemma related to your chosen career field
- ✓ **balance** multiple perspectives thoughtfully
- ✓ use relevant research methods and sources
- ✓ demonstrate excellent **knowledge** and understanding of the topic and awareness of its impact on the contexts, individuals and groups you have identified
- ✓ apply source material and correct use of subject-specific terminology and/or concepts
- ✓ draw relevant conclusions that are proficiently analysed and help support a personal position
- ✓ offer a sustained, reasoned argument supported effectively by evidence
- ✓ demonstrate your skill as a **thinker** by showing that you have critically evaluated research
- ✓ demonstrate that you have considered the impact of the dilemma and your position
- ✓ include consistent and accurate use of terminology as well as structural and stylistic conventions
- ✓ present ideas with coherence and consistency to support the reading/viewing of the project
- ✓ include accurate and consistent in-text citations as well as a correctly formatted bibliography or reference list
- ✓ comply with all format requirements.

> ## Learning journal entry
>
> ### Activity
>
> Use the checklist above to ensure you have met all the requirements for the reflective project. If any areas have not been addressed, reflect on the feedback you have been given to help you make any final revisions. Then use the descriptors for criteria A to D in Chapter 7 to self-assess your project.
>
> ### Reflect
>
> What final mark would you give yourself? Why?
>
> Is there anything you could still improve before you submit your project?

Completing and submitting your written reflection

Once you have completed your reflective project, you must create a final written reflection to submit alongside it. This is a written summary that must be submitted on the Reflective Project – Final Reflection Form (RP/FRF), and it is part of your formal assessment.

Your supervisor will give you a copy of the RP/FRF form. Get this in advance so that you can begin drafting your final reflection while your supervisor is reviewing the refined (but not final) draft of your reflective project. You can then finalise your written reflection after you complete and self-evaluate your project. You might want to draft your final written reflection in a word-processing document and proofread it carefully before copying it into the form.

Reflective and reflexive practice

While the final written reflection is completed at the end of your reflective project journey, reflective and reflexive practices should be intentional, active and on-going throughout the process.

You have been using this book to guide your learning journal entries, which have created a record of your reflections as you have progressed through the reflective project journey. Here in the final stage of the process, you can look back at your learning journal and use extracts from it to support your final written reflection. Your learning journal can also help you prepare for the viva voce.

Because your learning journal reflections were authentically recorded at different points in time, the entries used to create the final written reflection should be adapted rather than copied directly onto the form. Your goal is to create a coherent and holistic final observation that demonstrates different types of reflection: on your process, on your project and on your learning.

While there is no one 'right' approach to writing the final written reflection, the RP/FRF form is used to mark your project on Criterion E, so it should include the different types of reflection and reflexivity assessed there. In Chapter 2, you learned about these different types of reflection (metacognitive, process and critical) and reflexivity (self and critical). All these different types of reflection should be included in the RP/FRF form. As you did with your completed project, use the assessment criterion descriptors as a guide. Look back at Chapter 7 to remind yourself what questions you should ask yourself to evaluate your work for Criterion E, what successful work looks like and some tips you can use as a checklist. You can also look at the IB guidance for the reflective project to understand the full criterion.

Example

Reflective project research question: To what extent can graphic designers ethically take inspiration from existing designs while respecting intellectual property rights and promoting artistic integrity?

Career-related focus for the RP: Graphic design & Business

Final reflection:

Sample text	Commentary
When I first began considering topics for my reflective project, I was determined to select an issue that genuinely connected with my future career aspirations in graphic design. This was important to me because I knew that exploring something personally relevant would not only sustain my engagement throughout the lengthy research process but also provide insights that would help me navigate professional challenges responsibly. I chose to investigate Intellectual Property (IP) ethics in graphic design, particularly focusing on how businesses related to graphic design balance innovation protection with ethical considerations around access and cultural appropriation.	This reflection establishes immediate strong career relevance with specific professional implications. It demonstrates metacognitive reflection by explicitly connecting the student's ethical dilemma selection to future professional development, showing strategic thinking about their learning objectives.
My initial approach to research felt quite methodical. I heavily relied on Google Scholar as my primary database because it provided credible and valuable resources, including case studies, academic articles, and expert opinions that I needed to understand the complexity of IP ethics. However, I quickly realised that I couldn't make solid conclusions without deeper critical analysis, so I decided to incorporate the OPVL method to systematically evaluate my findings and ensure I was approaching sources with appropriate scepticism.	This is an example of excellent process reflection with specific methodological awareness. This demonstrates critical reflection by recognising limitations in initial approach and adapting methodology accordingly, showing intellectual maturity and self-awareness.
One of the most challenging aspects of this project emerged during my interim research phase when I encountered a particularly complex case study with a highly debatable outcome. It was difficult for me to analyse this case without falling into bias, and I found myself struggling to reach conclusions that weren't influenced by my personal perspectives. To address this challenge, I had to consciously question my own opinions, conduct additional research to expose myself to different viewpoints, and continuously refine my scope of research to maintain objectivity. This process of self-examination was uncomfortable but crucial for developing my critical thinking and reflective skills.	This reflection exemplifies self-reflexivity through honest examination of bias and deliberate strategies for addressing the student's own bias and assumptions, which demonstrates critical self-examination of their own thinking processes.
The feedback I received from my supervisor during our regular meetings proved invaluable in guiding my research direction. When I expressed uncertainty about managing my potential bias as someone interested in business innovation in the graphic design area, my supervisor	This demonstrates critical reflection as it shows how the student responded constructively to feedback by adapting their research approach.

encouraged me to actively seek out perspectives from different stakeholders - including inventors, competitors, indigenous communities, and consumers. This guidance led me to investigate the historical and cultural differences in intellectual property enforcement across various regions, which gave me entirely new perspectives on how context shapes ethical practices in businesses related to graphic design.	
Throughout the research and writing process, my understanding of the ethical dilemma evolved significantly. Initially, I approached the topic believing there would be a relatively straightforward answer to my research question about balancing innovation protection with ethical access. However, as I delved deeper into the various stakeholder perspectives and analysed multiple case studies, I came to realise the profound depth and complexity surrounding intellectual property ethics, particularly in graphic design. This realisation fundamentally changed how I view business decisions - I now understand that ethical dilemmas in professional contexts rarely have simple solutions and require careful consideration of competing values and interests.	This reflection provides compelling evidence of genuine learning evolution of the student's perspective, and demonstrates metacognitive reflection on learning process. It shows intellectual development in recognising increased complexity in the student's ethical dilemma.
This project has had a measurable impact on my skill development. I have notably improved my research capabilities, time management, and organisational skills, as well as my ability to evaluate sources critically and engage in more reflective and analytical thinking. Beyond these practical skills, the project has broadened my perspective on what it means to be an ethical business professional in the graphic design field. Understanding how intellectual property decisions can affect innovation, cultural preservation, and economic development has prepared me to approach similar dilemmas in my future career with greater nuance and consideration for multiple stakeholders.	This demonstrates process and critical reflection by examining the effectiveness of the research approach and project outcomes. The student shows self-reflexivity by demonstrating mature analytical capability about their research process and how to approach similar projects in the future.
Perhaps most importantly, this research has shaped my view on the necessity of robust ethical frameworks in business practice. I now recognise that professionals in my chosen field will regularly encounter situations where legal compliance and ethical responsibility may not perfectly align, and where cultural sensitivity and global awareness are just as important as protecting commercial interests. This awareness will undoubtedly guide my future work and decision-making as I enter the business and graphic design world. The insights I've gained through this process extend beyond my personal & professional development. I believe that increased understanding of intellectual property ethics could significantly influence how businesses related to graphic design approach innovation and cultural engagement. When professionals are equipped with frameworks for navigating these complex ethical considerations, it can lead to more responsible business practices, better protection of cultural heritage, and more equitable access to innovations that benefit society broadly.	This connects to critical reflection as well as self-reflexivity by demonstrating the student's ability to think about their own learning process and consider how their insights might influence broader professional practice. It shows sophisticated understanding of how individual learning connects to systemic change.

Learning journal entry

Reflection

Were you able to recognise the different types of reflection?

Can you identify similar types of reflection in your own learning journal entries?

Remember

If you do not submit the RP/FRF or if it is left blank, 0 marks will be awarded for Criterion E. The RP/FRF must also be completed in the same language as your project otherwise it will not be awarded any marks.

The maximum total word count for the final reflective statement on the RP/FRF is 1,000 words. Examiners will not read or assess beyond this limit.

If you went over 3,000 words in your reflective project, you might have fewer than 1,000 words for your final reflection. Reflections that are too short usually do not include enough of the different types of reflection and reflexivity to score well on Criterion E, so make sure the balance between the two components is right.

Use the questions in the diagrams below to prompt your thinking as you prepare your final written reflection.

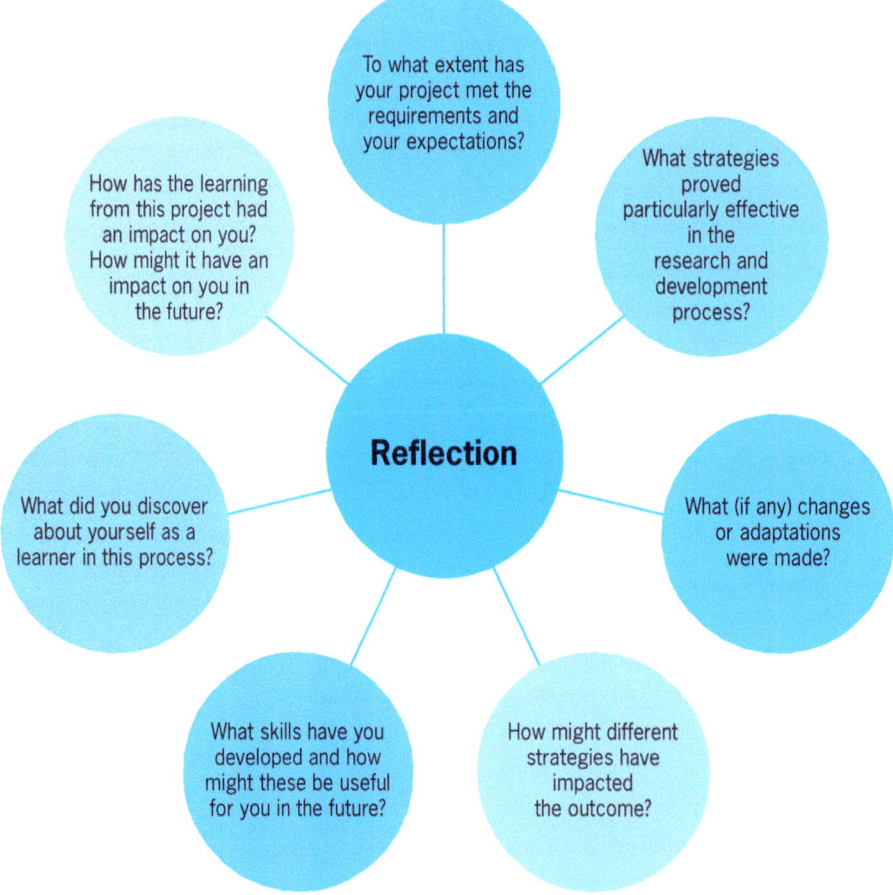

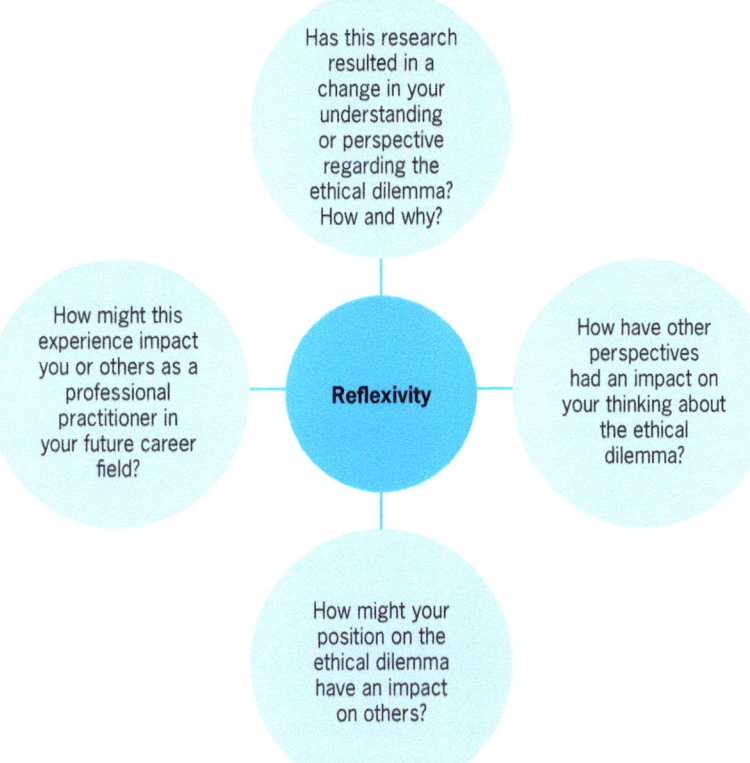

Learning journal entry

Activity

Once you have written your final reflection, use the checklist below to ensure you have included all the different types of reflection and reflexivity, and that you have fully addressed the descriptors of Criterion E.

- ✓ Skills and knowledge gained throughout the learning journey.
- ✓ Important choices, challenges or decisions made during the planning, research and development process.
- ✓ Insights and new understandings that resulted from researching and developing the project.
- ✓ How peer or reflective project supervisor feedback had an impact on your thinking, actions or choices.
- ✓ An evaluation of your project's execution and outcome.
- ✓ Any changes in your perspective on the ethical dilemma or issues related to it.
- ✓ Experiences and insights that could shape future thinking, whether your own or within your career field.

If you think anything is missing, review your learning journal to find excerpts or examples that will help you make any revisions.

Preparing for and participating in your viva voce

The viva voce serves as a culminating moment to celebrate the completion of your project. It allows you to showcase your comprehensive understanding, critical thinking and personal growth from across your entire learning journey. For your supervisor, the viva voce also helps to confirm the authenticity of your work by considering your ability to explain your learning process and to analyse and evaluate your final project.

In reflecting on your entire reflective project journey, both in your final written reflection and during the viva voce with your supervisor, you should include thoughts about the process, your self-evaluation of the final completed product, reflections on how the skills and the learning you have developed have contributed to your personal growth, and how your new understanding of the ethical dilemma might impact you as a future practitioner in your career field.

The viva voce may be led by your supervisor, but you can prepare for it by reviewing your final written reflection. You might even take some ownership and initiative by leading with a few key reflections based on excerpts from your learning journal to prompt conversation.

The viva voce will be like your final written reflection, but because it is a conversation with your supervisor, it is likely to be more thorough – although perhaps less stressful! The conversation might include:

- the focus of your reflective project, and how it relates to your career interest
- how you identified your ethical dilemma, and why it sparked your interest
- your initial thoughts or biases about the ethical dilemma
- the research you undertook, including your reasoning for the approach you chose
- the research findings you gathered
- the format option you chose, and your reasoning for choosing it
- reflections on challenges encountered during your research and development process
- a review of your overall understanding of your ethical dilemma, and how it was manifested in your personal position and final product
- how your perspective or understanding might have changed, and why
- a review of the skills you developed across your RP learning journey
- a review of your final project including both limitations and strengths
- your personal performance and development throughout your reflective project learning journey
- what you learned from undertaking the reflective project, and how it might have an impact on your future career or education.

Whether you take a leading role, or you simply respond to your supervisor's questions, giving reflective and insightful responses will demonstrate your ability to critically analyse your final project, reflect on your own development, and **communicate** your self-discovery along the learning journey. You do not need to study or plan extensively for the viva voce – after all, you know better than anyone what your experience was – but it will give you confidence if you feel prepared!

Learning journal entry

Choose a few sentence stems from each section below to structure your responses as you prepare for the viva voce.

Process-related:

- My research question was…, and the ethical dilemma I focused on was….
- I chose this topic/ethical dilemma because….
- Initially, I hoped to discover….
- The key findings from my research were…, and they helped me gain a deeper understanding of the ethical dilemma by….
- The conclusions I have drawn about my ethical dilemma are….
- Having completed my project, the additional discoveries I have made are….
- Reflecting on my research process, the main challenges I encountered were….
- The methodology I used for my research was….
- I decided to approach it this way because….
- The limitations of my research approach were….
- Some additional questions I have about the issue that could lead to further investigation are….
- The challenges I encountered were…. I overcame them by….
- The unexpected or contradictory findings during my research were…, and I navigated and worked through them by….
- The things I would have done differently in my research process were…, because….
- During my research, what I discovered about the complexity of ethical decision-making is….
- Throughout the research process, my understanding of the ethical dilemma evolved from… to….

Project-related:

- The ethical frameworks or theories I utilised to analyse the ethical dilemma were…. They helped to inform my understanding and conclusions by….
- If I were to conduct further research, the specific areas or aspects I would explore would be…, because….
- The most significant insights I gained from my reflective project were… and they changed my perspective on….

- Engaging with the reflective project deepened my understanding of the ethical complexities within my chosen career field by….

Personal growth-related:

- Engaging with this ethical dilemma influenced my way of thinking about related issues or topics by…because….
- Insights I gained about the dilemma include…. Insights about my career field include…. Insights I had about myself are….
- The most valuable skills or knowledge that I have developed throughout my reflective project learning journey are…. I envision applying them in my future career or education by….
- Reflecting on my personal growth, the things I have learned about myself through engaging with the reflective project are….

Impact-related:

- Looking back at my reflective project learning journey, the most rewarding aspect for me was….
- The most challenging aspect of my learning journey was…, and I overcame it by….
- I think this experience of completing the reflective project will impact my future work/studies in terms of ethical decision making by….
- The advice I would give to future learners undertaking the reflective project or embarking on a similar research process are….
- My reflective project contributes to my understanding of professional ethics by demonstrating … , and highlighting the importance of ….

Authenticating your work

At the conclusion of the viva voce, you and your supervisor need to sign your RP/FRF form to confirm that the work you are submitting is your own and does not contain any instances of plagiarism. Your signature on the form means that you are guaranteeing that you have cited or documented anyone else's ideas – this is a final confirmation of your academic integrity.

Once you have signed and dated the form, you cannot retract or modify your project. This is why it is important for you to have used the criteria and checklists to ensure you have included all requirements and that you have provided all your documents complete and in the correct format for submission.

Learning journal entry

Activity

Use the checklist below to ensure you have completed all the requirements and have the correct documents to submit your final project.

- ✓ Your project is in the correct format required by the IB (for example, .doc, .docx, .pdf, .jpg, .jpeg, .png, .rtf, .m4a, .mp3, .mp4, .mov or .m4v depending on the format).
- ✓ If you submitted an audio or audio-visual project, you have included a transcript in the appendix.
- ✓ If you submitted a visual, audio or audio-visual project, you have included an additional written format for any extra information and explanations about how your use of music, image, and so on, contribute to your project.
- ✓ You have used a consistent and accurate method for citing and referencing your sources.
- ✓ There are no instances of plagiarism or collusion. Your work is your own.
- ✓ Your final reflection is on the RP/FRF form.
- ✓ The form is signed and dated by you and your supervisor.

If you can check off every item on this list, you can feel confident that you have done your part. Your supervisor and Career-related Programme coordinator will now be responsible for uploading your reflective project for assessment by the IB.

Congratulations – you have officially completed your reflective project learning journey! Take a moment to celebrate your learning. You have developed research skills and refined your communication skills, you have learned to receive and respond to feedback, and you have met and overcome challenges to see a lengthy independent project through to the end. These are skills you can rely on in the future as you complete other projects at university or in your future career. You should be proud of the work you have done!

Key takeaways: Chapter 9

- You can strengthen your final submission by using feedback from your supervisor and the criteria guidelines to revise, improve and complete your project.
- As part of project completion, you must self-evaluate your project using the criteria.
- You can use the reflections you have been keeping in your learning journal to help you write your final reflection and prepare for the viva voce.
- Once you have checked that you have met all the requirements and completed all the required documents, remember to celebrate your achievement!

Chapter 10 – Your questions answered

> **This chapter includes answers about the following:**
> - Learning journal and reflective practice
> - Ethical dilemmas and analysis
> - Research methods and sources
> - Project structure and requirements
> - Project management and organisation
> - Personal position
> - The use of AI
> - Supervision and feedback

Learning journal and reflective practice
Using templates

Is there a template I can use to organise my learning journal entries?

Different methods can help you catalogue your entries effectively. For example, if you use:

- a physical journal, create clear tags and labels for different sections and purposes
- a digital journal, consider setting up menu tabs and folders for easy navigation.

On the following page there is an example of how you could set up a digital reflective project learning journal. The table of contents can be organised to follow the learning journey. Each tab in the table can be hyperlinked to a specific page or folder that corresponds to that section of your learning journal.

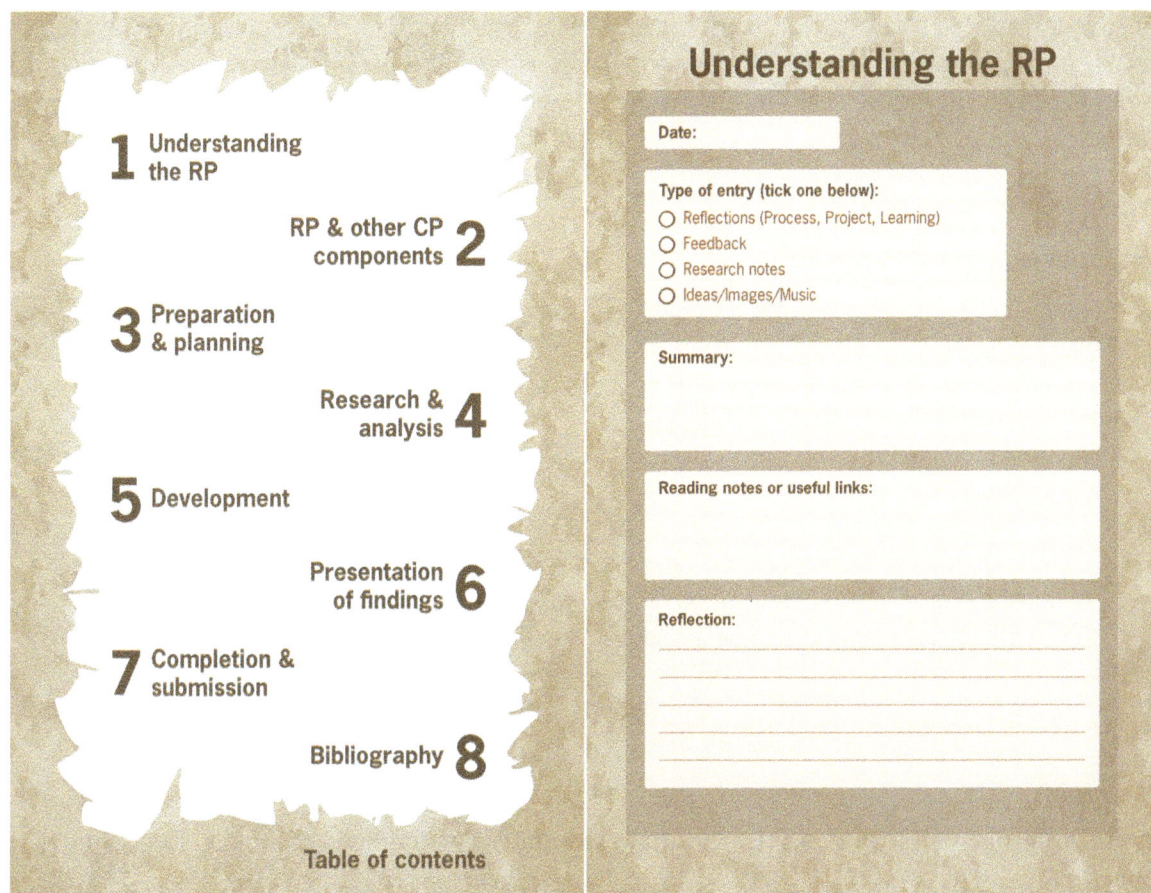

Regardless of format, the following tips may be helpful:

- Timestamp each journal entry and include a summary.
- Use icons or colour-coding to categorise different types of entries.
- Organise entries into categories such as: Reflections; Feedback; Research notes; Images / Soundtracks; Reflections.
- Group reflections into the following sections: Process; Project; Learning.
- Tag or highlight entries by reflection type:
    - Metacognition
    - Process reflection
    - Critical reflection
    - Self-reflexivity
    - Critical reflexivity.

Including reflection and reflexivity

How many types of reflection and reflexivity do I have to include in my learning journal?

You should include a variety of authentic reflections you have along the way – in so doing you will likely address all the different types of reflection and reflexivity. However, your final written reflection (using the RP/FRF form) requires you to show evidence of metacognition, process reflection, critical reflection, self-reflexivity and critical reflexivity, so you should be conscious of including all these types of reflection in your learning journal at appropriate points. One way to do this while keeping your reflections natural is to go back through your learning journal as you enter each new phase of your journey to review your reflections from the previous phase and tag or highlight them to indicate the type of reflection or reflexivity used. This will make it easier for you to identify relevant excerpts from your learning journal to use in your final written reflection as well as the viva voce.

Assessing the learning journal

Is my learning journal assessed?

The learning journal will not be assessed by the IB. It is intended for your own reflection and note-taking during your reflective project learning journey. Your school may ask to review it as a progress check, but it should not be graded. Your final written reflection, however, *is* assessed as part of your final project using Criterion E, which is focused solely on reflection.

> **References**
> - Chapter 2 explains the purpose and requirements of your learning journal and outlines Criterion E.
> - Chapter 2 explains the different types of reflection and reflexivity.
> - Chapter 9 explains what should be included in the final written reflection and the viva voce.

Ethical dilemmas and analysis

Applying theories and frameworks

I'm not sure which ethical theories or frameworks apply to my ethical dilemma. What should I do?

You are not expected to be an expert in ethical theories, but you should be familiar with some of the basic frameworks such as deontology, utilitarianism, virtue ethics and ethics of care. You will probably have learned about these in your personal and professional skills course or one of the other Career-related Programme core components. The main thing to remember is that an ethical dilemma puts into conflict at least two different values (for example, public rights vs individual rights, justice vs injustice, common good vs private or corporate benefit). If you can identify these and the main stakeholders, you will be able to guide your research and use your findings to sufficiently address your dilemma in a balanced way. If you are still struggling to see how ethics applies to your chosen dilemma, it may be that your project is more focused on a general research question than an ethical dilemma, in which case you will need to rethink your approach. Remember, you can always share your ideas and concerns with your supervisor.

Being clear and concise

How can I comprehensively analyse my ethical dilemma without being too complex?

Ethical issues are complex, but you do need to analyse your dilemma so it is clear, connected and concise. While your research may lead you down many paths, as you prepare to analyse and communicate your research, try to narrow your focus into two or three conflicting values and focus just on the stakeholders who are most affected. You can also refer to the ethical analysis tools and methods introduced in Chapters 5 and 6 to help you organise and categorise your research notes and thoughts. As you develop your outline, identify your key points and their supporting documentation to keep your discussion focused and connected.

Giving your own opinion

I find ethics complicated and I often feel overwhelmed when trying to determine what is right and what is wrong. How can I avoid this when producing my reflective project?

An ethical dilemma will never have a single clear answer, because the perspectives and values involved in it will be different for different stakeholders. That feeling of uncertainty just means you can empathise with other perspectives – which is one of the goals of an IB education! The aim of the reflective project is to try and understand the perspectives, values and impact of the dilemma on the stakeholders, and then – based on your own perspective and values, and the evidence you have seen – *give your own opinion* on the best resolution to the dilemma, and explain how you came to that conclusion. Try putting yourself into the position of a practitioner of your future profession and let that help guide your thinking.

Changing your dilemma

Can I change my ethical dilemma midway through the reflective project?

It is possible to change your ethical dilemma – but not advisable. Switching the focus means you will have less time than you need to thoroughly explore and analyse your dilemma. That's why it's important to spend time at the start really thinking things through. If you have several interesting ideas to begin with, share them with your supervisor, explore them all just enough to know which one seems most suitable for your project. However, if you get really stuck or simply can't find enough information on the dilemma you chose, talk to your supervisor and together weigh the pros and cons of revising your research question or completely switching your dilemma given your time frame.

> **References**
> - Chapter 3 provides an overview of different ethical theories and frameworks and explains what an ethical dilemma is.
> - Chapter 4 helps you understand how to identify an ethical dilemma and turn it into a research question.
> - Chapter 6 provides strategies for how to organise and analyse your research, including different aspects of your dilemma and varying stakeholders' perspectives.

Research methods and sources

Exploring different angles

How many sources, contexts and perspectives should I focus on?

There is no set number required by the IB, but you are expected to explore your ethical dilemma from several different angles. You will research the different contexts in which the dilemma manifests itself and the perspectives of the stakeholders involved, so the numbers of these will vary depending on the dilemma, as will the number of sources. For example, if there are three key stakeholders, you will probably want to find sources that share the perspectives of each of these stakeholders. If you are looking at a source that focuses on one specific stakeholder's opinion, that source is likely to be biased so to ensure your research is balanced, you will want to find additional sources that give alternative perspectives.

Adjusting your research

Can I adjust my research question midway to fit what I have found through my research?

Your research question is the basis for what you are exploring. Your findings do not need to alter your research question, but they very well may alter your thinking. This is fine – improved or changed understanding is the purpose of research. However, if your findings are giving you second thoughts about your original research question (for example, you now think your question may be too broad, or that there are perspectives you had not originally considered), talk to your supervisor about refining or improving your research question.

Using primary research

Is primary research mandatory?

There are advantages to both primary and secondary research, but you should think practically about your timeframe, the nature and scope of your research question, and the resources at your disposal. You might start by checking existing primary sources and then decide whether there is sufficient information, or whether it makes more sense for you to conduct your own primary research. You can also combine primary and secondary research to ensure you have thoroughly addressed your ethical dilemma in a balanced way. Once you have given consideration to both types of research, develop your research plan and share it with your supervisor for feedback, so that you can adjust your approach as needed.

> ## References
> - Chapter 2 explains the requirements of the reflective project.
> - Chapter 5 and 6 explains the research process and provides strategies for analysing your sources.
> - Chapter 7 provides sample formats for citing and referencing your research.

Project structure and requirements

Creating additional content

Is the additional written content always required for projects in the non-written formats, and does it count towards the main word limit?

Audio and audio-visual formats require a transcript to be submitted as part of the appendix just in case of technology problems, but the appendix does *not* count in the total word count. All formats require a bibliography, and citations or references must be properly documented; the non-written formats have some additional requirements. Audio and audio-visual formats are submitted in a different format to written or visual projects. The visual format requires annotations for each image so that the examiner can understand what the images are and how they tell the story of your dilemma and your research. For all non-written formats, you should also explain why you chose your images or music, and these additional texts *do* contribute to the total word count. You should consider all requirements before deciding on the format of your reflective project to ensure you are able to develop a successful project.

> ## References
> - Chapter 7 outlines the requirements for each of the different format options.

Project management and organisation

Organising research

Is there a recommended template for organising research in a way that will make writing my reflective project more efficient?

Keeping your research organised from the very beginning will help you in all the following phases of the reflective project journey. An annotated bibliography helps you to track your research, which makes it easier to identify the sources and citations you want to use later. Keep all your research notes and reflections in your learning journal so that everything is in one place, and tag or highlight them to make sure they are easy to find when you are ready to use them. If you adopt one of the analysis templates suggested in Chapter 5, you can use your responses to lay out the key ideas for both your project development and your oral presentation. It is also advisable to begin your project development with an outline of the key ideas resulting from your research. By outlining the key points, you can keep your focus and communicate your ideas in a clear, concise and coherent manner. All these things will help you to be as efficient as possible during the research and development phases.

> **References**
> - Chapter 5 explains the research and analysis process. Several of the strategies and templates shared there can support the development of your project.
> - Chapter 7 explains how to develop your project effectively beginning with an outline.

Personal position

Providing a 'call to action'

Does my personal position always need a 'call to action' or specific solution?

While ethical dilemmas do not have a clear solution, they can be resolved by making an ethical decision that reflects your own perspectives and values. Your reflective project must include a statement of your personal position on the dilemma and your reasoning or evidence for that conclusion. While some formats lend themselves to a call to action, this is not necessarily required. For example, if you are writing a dissertation-style essay, you would explain your dilemma, analyse the different contexts and perspectives, identify possible solutions and explain your personal position. This type of essay usually takes an objective approach, so a call to action may not be appropriate here. However, a call to action is a typical convention for speeches, so if your project takes this format, you could suggest what action your target audience could take to resolve the dilemma in alignment with your position.

Explaining your position

Do I need to argue my personal position and prove with research how it is the correct resolution to the ethical dilemma, or is the goal of the reflective project to take a more holistic look and discuss my perspective in relation to other viewpoints?

The goal of the reflective project is to thoroughly explore an ethical dilemma through the various contexts and perspectives of impacted stakeholders, then to make an ethical decision based on the research you have done and how it aligns with your personal values or thinking. You must discuss differing viewpoints in a fair and balanced way, explaining why different stakeholders have a particular perspective, and perhaps whether or why you agree or disagree with them.

Remember that, by its nature, there is no one 'correct' solution to an ethical dilemma. Therefore, you do not have to persuade anyone that you are right; you simply must explain your position, why you think that way, and how you arrived at your conclusion. However, depending on the format you are using, the tone or language you use might be persuasive. For example, if you are putting yourself in the role of a consultant writing a business proposal based on case studies, or if you are writing a letter to a professional regulating body, or if you are making a speech, you should come across as both logical and persuasive so that others can understand and perhaps agree with your position.

Offering balance

How can I offer a balanced discussion of perspectives while still demonstrating my own opinion?

It is important to provide a balanced discussion, sharing different perspectives in a way that shows you understand their reasoning. You might consider explaining what causes each stakeholder to have their particular perspective (for example cultural or social values, how they are negatively or positively impacted by the dilemma and how that might influence their perspective). However, once you have done this, you should share your own conclusion and clearly state how your research findings and your personal values helped you to arrive at your position. You might agree with certain aspects of the other perspectives, or your position may align with one of the specific perspectives you explored – or it may be an entirely different viewpoint. Whichever it is, make sure you fairly discuss everyone's perspective before stating your own.

> ## References
> - Chapter 6 offers guidance on how to analyse and synthesise your research to reach a personal position.

The use of AI

Brainstorming with AI

Can I use AI to help brainstorm or outline my project?

You can use AI as a support tool, but not as a co-developer of your project. That means you can use it to brainstorm ideas about ethical issues related to your career interest and relevant contexts or stakeholders, but then you must do the research to gather and analyse the information yourself. You can use AI to find templates or get a general idea for your format, but you need to be the one who creates your outline and writes the draft. Even if you are only using AI for brainstorming, you should make sure to note it in your learning journal so that you can document it as evidence of your academic integrity. If you use anything created by AI (a paragraph or an image or other ideas) you must cite it as a source, just like you would any other source. If you are unsure, consult with your supervisor or your school librarian for advice. Your reflective project coordinator will also have access to all the academic integrity rules for the IB, and they should be able to answer any specific questions you might have about your school's or the IB's policies.

> ## References
> - Chapter 5 includes details about how to use AI and other resources ethically and responsibly.
> - Chapter 7 includes important information about academic integrity.

Supervision and feedback

Asking friends for feedback

Can I ask my friends or family members to look at my drafts and give me feedback?

Your supervisor should be your main source of support and feedback. However, as they are limited to 3–6 hours of total support, you can seek additional opportunities for feedback when needed. Peer feedback can be very useful, particularly when discussing your early ideas or to get clarity in your thinking; this is why there is a peer feedback opportunity following your presentation. You can also get feedback or ask questions of other knowledgeable people. For example, your school librarian may be able to offer advice on research skills or particular sources, and a language teacher might be able to offer ideas about some of the structural and stylistic conventions of your chosen format. But the reflective project is designed to be an independent project, so ultimately your work must be completely your own. There are severe consequences for collusion or other breaches of academic integrity, so while you should feel free to get general feedback, do not ask someone to alter or 'correct' your project for you.

Dealing with conflicting feedback

Sometimes my supervisor tells me one thing, then another person tells me something completely different. How do I handle conflicting feedback?

Although it can be useful to get feedback from several sources, your supervisor should be your main source for this. However, an important part of the reflective project is deciding whether or how to act on that feedback. Always consider whether the person offering feedback has expertise in the area or subject. Then, think about whether acting on their feedback will improve your project. If you are uncertain about feedback, always clarify your understanding before deciding to make any changes. Ultimately, it is *your* decision. Be sure, too, to record any feedback as well as any action taken in your learning journal. This will help you keep a record both for reflection purposes and for documentation of your academic integrity.

Approaching your supervisor

My school's timeline means that I have to submit my first draft for supervisor feedback; after that there is no opportunity to get feedback on later drafts. What should I do in this situation?

Your supervisor can only provide detailed formal comments on one full draft, and your school might dictate that this needs to be the first draft. However, you can still approach your supervisor for general feedback when creating subsequent drafts. You will also receive feedback after your oral presentation. If you have a specific question about a small section of your draft where your supervisor suggested more work, or about the feedback received after your presentation, you can approach them to discuss the revisions you have made or to seek clarification on any specific feedback you received.

> ## References
> - Chapter 1 offers advice about how to work with your supervisor.
> - Chapter 2 suggests ways of responding to feedback.
> - Chapter 9 provides suggestions about using feedback from your presentation and your supervisor to complete your final project.

Glossary

abstract: a summary of the contents of a piece of academic research

aggregator: something that collects related pieces of information from a variety of sources

AI tool: software that uses artificial intelligence algorithms to solve problems and perform tasks

analysis: the process of considering something carefully or using statistical methods to understand or explain it

anecdote: a short, sometimes amusing, account of something that has happened

articulate: to express or explain your ideas, thoughts or reasoning in a clear, distinct way

assumption: something that is accepted as being true or sure to happen, without any proof

autonomy: the ability and freedom to make your own decisions rather than being told what to do by someone else; respecting autonomy means allowing people to control their own lives

beneficence: the act of doing good and helping others to make their lives better

bias: a tendency to prefer one person, thing or idea to another, and to favour that; bias can affect how you see and judge something

bibliography: a list of articles, books and other sources that have been referenced in a piece of work

call to action: an exhortation to do something to achieve an aim or deal with a problem

cite: to refer and give credit to someone else's work

collation: the process of gathering, organising and bringing together information about your topic from different sources

collusion: cooperation between two parties that is against the rules or illegal

common good: something that is available and accessible to everyone in a community or society, and which improves the wellbeing of all people, not just a few individuals

context: the circumstances, events and settings that give meaning to what is learned; context helps make sense of the world by considering the factors that influence what is seen, heard or read

contextualisation: placing an idea within its relevant background or framework, showing how it fits into the larger picture

conventions: the typical style and structure demonstrated in specific types of writing or presentations; this might include features such as headings and subheadings, the level of formality in the language used, as well as the grammar and punctuation used

critical thinking: the process of examining a subject or idea carefully and critically, without allowing yourself to be influenced by opinions or feelings

cultural appropriation: the act of taking or using things from a culture that is not your own, without demonstrating understanding or respect for that culture

data: a collection or series of facts, observations or measurements, often presented in the form of numbers or letters

dataset: a collection of separate sets of information that is treated as a single unit by a computer

dialogue tagging: also known as speech tags, these are phrases that are used to break up sections of written dialogue (for example, 'he said')

diction: choice of words or the manner of expression

dissertation: a long essay on a particular subject

enunciation: the act of pronouncing words or parts of words clearly

ethical decision-making: the process of choosing a course of action when faced with moral questions or dilemmas; this involves evaluating different options based on your ethical values and considering the consequences for all people affected, to arrive at a responsible and justifiable choice

ethical dilemma: an ethical issue in which someone must choose between conflicting values or actions, each with its own drawbacks; while all ethical dilemmas are ethical issues, not all ethical issues necessarily present a dilemma

ethical thinking: the process of carefully considering right and wrong, and using your values to guide your decisions; this involves critically examining your own beliefs and the possible effects of choices on others to act responsibly and fairly

ethics: moral beliefs, rules and principles about right and wrong

evaluate: to assess or judge the quality or importance of something

executive summary: a written account that gives an overview of the main points in a longer document, such as a report or plan

explicit: describing something that is stated openly, so it is clear and exact

expository essay: an essay that aims to inform a reader about something, or to explain something to them

footage: the extent of film material that has been shot

formative assessment: a range of formal and informal assessment processes carried out by teachers to assess your progress; formative assessment is designed to give you feedback to help you improve as you go along

global context: the big picture of what is happening around the world; how different places and people are connected and the common issues or challenges that affect many countries and communities

greater good: help for most people in society and decisions benefit the majority, even if this might not be the best for every single person; closely associated with the utilitarian branch of ethics

holistic: dealing with the whole of something, not just a part of it, considering all influencing factors

human rights: the basic rights that many societies believe that all people should have, and in which individuals and organisations such as governments should not interfere

implicit: describing something that is suggested but which is not communicated directly, so it must be understood by considering other information, including its context

informed consent: permission given by someone who understands fully what they are agreeing to

integrity: a quality characterised by being honest and sticking to moral principles

intercultural understanding: the ability to recognise and respect cultural differences and interact effectively with people from different cultural backgrounds

local context: the specific features and conditions of a particular place or community, such as its geography, culture, economy, environment and politics

methodology: the research approaches, frameworks, and strategies used in a particular discipline

mixed approach: an approach to research that combines primary and secondary research; you collect your own data as well as using existing information to get a fuller, clearer picture of your research question

moral agent: a person who can distinguish right from wrong, make moral judgements and be held accountable for their actions

narrative: an account, report or story of events or experiences

non-maleficence: the duty that people have, especially medical practitioners, to 'do no harm' when making decisions; it requires consideration of how actions might hurt or cause injury to people and what steps can be taken to avoid that

open-access: referring to publications that are freely available online, with no financial, legal or technical restriction on their availability or use

paraphrase: to express what someone else has written or said using your own words

perspective: a particular way of thinking about something, especially one that is influenced by someone's own beliefs or experiences

plagiarism: the act of using someone else's words or ideas and not crediting them

point of view: a mental viewpoint or attitude

primary research: the process of collecting original data to answer specific questions relating to a study; primary research may be conducted through surveys, interviews, focus groups, observations, experiments or case studies

reflexive: the ability to examine your own thoughts, feelings, beliefs, attitudes and behaviours; in the context of the reflective project, it means being aware of your own assumptions and biases, and understanding how these influence your responses and decisions

repository: a place where things are stored, often things that contain knowledge and information

right to privacy: the fundamental right that people must be free from unwarranted intrusion or interference in their personal space, communications and information

secondary research: the process of analysing existing data that others have already collected; often carried out to gather background information before starting primary research; methods include literature reviews, government reports, books, academic journals, online databases and news articles

segment: sections of film or television footage that each focus on a particular thing

sponsor: an individual, organisation, or group that provides financial, technical, or other type of support for a publication, research project, or event; knowing the sponsor can help determine potential influences or biases in the source

stakeholder: a person, group or community that is affected by or has an interest in something; in the reflective project, this means everyone who might be impacted, whether they are in your own community or in other parts of the world

structural elements: the features that characterise how a piece of writing or other presentation format is organised, such as formatting, chapter headings, titles and subtitles, page breaks, dialogue tagging, grammar, punctuation, spelling, capitalisation, paragraphing and citation styles

summative assessment: an assessment at the end of a learning process designed to evaluate how much you have achieved and how well you understand the subject matter

survey: a questionnaire used to gather information by asking a sample of people a series of specific questions

syntax: the way that words are put together to make sentences

synthesis: the combination of separate elements into a whole

systemic: relating to things that are about or affect a whole system

terminology: the specific words and phrases that are commonly used in a particular subject, field or type of writing; knowing and using the correct terminology allows you to communicate your ideas clearly and accurately

theoretical: referring to things that exist only as an idea, rather than being real or actually happening

tone: the general attitude or feeling of a piece of writing

transition: word or phrase that indicates the relationship between ideas in a piece of writing

transparency: being open, honest and clear about what you are doing, allowing others to understand your actions and decisions, to build trust

utilitarianism: the idea that the morally correct course of action is the one that produces benefit for the greatest number of people

viva voce: (Latin 'with living voice') the final session or 'interview' with your reflective project supervisor, in which you will discuss your project, the process you went through, what you learned and your personal growth

voiceover: a piece of narration in a film or television piece, where the speaker does not appear on camera